GUNS & MOSES

God's Formula for Wielding Power and Shielding the Powerless

DR. JEFFREY L. SEIF

Guns & Moses

God's Formula for Wielding Power
and Shielding the Powerless

ISBN 978-1-930749-03-0

Dedicated to my fellow peace officers.

May God grant you
strength, wisdom, and protection
as you labor to keep the peace
in our troubled world.

Table of Contents

Table of Contents

Table of Contents

Introduction

God and War

Discoveries associated with categorizing, corralling, and domesticating manageable livestock, along with the seasonal harvesting of crops, had a profound impact on humankind's early development. Initially, many primitive people are said to have banded together in small familial groups from which they eked out livings following and hunting fast-moving herds. Through new ranching and farming technologies, however, many achieved success by saying "goodbye" to the small, mobile hunting parties and "hello" to the cultivation of lands and the management of crops and livestock. In the process of learning to steward resources, and by means of men's forging alliances with each other to secure their respective ranch holdings, civilization evolved.

The human story began in ancient Mesopotamia, a fertile expanse of land sometimes referred to as the "cradle of civilization," situated between the Tigris and Euphrates rivers. There, in what we call the "Fertile Crescent," the biblical drama is understood to have begun in the most verdant place of all: a lush, garden paradise called "Eden" (Gen. 2:10-17).

1

Paradise was lost shortly after it was found, however, as things went swiftly awry. Bested by their greedy impulses, Adam and Eve were eventually expelled from Eden (Gen. 3:23a) and given the mandate to attend to the Earth's development in the rough and inhospitable world outside (v. 23b).

Of the dispossessed couple's first recorded sons, Cain engaged in crop management (Gen. 4:2b-3), whereas Abel favored tending to livestock (v. 2a). Both types, farmers and ranchers, continued reproducing genetically and producing materially. Despite abounding jealousies and tensions, innovations within both agriculture and animal husbandry created personal wealth, stimulated the pioneering spirit, and intoxicated many with prospects for grand success in life. Humans built farms, cities, and towers (Gen. 11:4).

Teeming with life and possibility, the "Fertile Crescent" beckoned to many who hoped to secure prime real estate in the expansive area and employ the new technologies. Abraham was one such person. The Bible's first Hebrew began his west coast "gold rush" in Ur of the Chaldeans, in the Fertile Crescent's far eastern sector (Gen. 11:31). Abraham then ventured westward, to Syria and then to Canaan/Israel—with a brief detour in Egypt, owing to famine (Gen. 12:4-5, 10).

A bold sort, Abraham ventured where few dared to go—to what was considered the end of the Earth—in the interest of securing a new life in a relatively untapped part of the virgin world. Like any other man, he would have wanted his gutsy endeavors to meet with good success.

Aspirations of somehow becoming "great," his offspring somehow becoming "blessed," and his enemies somehow being "cursed" would have moved him and made the venture's risks somehow worth the effort. However, God,

Introduction

and not just gold, drove Abraham: he was propelled by a religious vision, more than pure economics—and his religious faith kept him going. Though tested by abundant hardships, his faith kept him focused as he quested for a preferred future in the strange new world. With God as his guide and by his side, he went west at a time when his private world dawned simultaneously with the broader new world (Gen. 15:1-6; 22:1ff—"ff" means "and following").

The hazardous frontier was no place for the spineless. Other nomadic types making similar bids to secure places in the untapped lands would have pressured *Abraham and his fledgling clan to develop strong soldiering skills* (see Gen. 14:1-16), and necessity would call them time and again to use those skills.

Guided by a religiously inspired sense of destiny, and believing that God accompanied him into life's battles, Abraham blessed the Lord in return for his military success (vv. 17-20). He seems to have instilled in his descendants a respect for the God that he understood to be the strong protector of their persons, their newly acquired property, and their developing way of life (Gen. 12:1-3; 15:1ff).

Abraham's faith premise was rather simple: *Abraham's children could become a mighty people because theirs was a mighty God.* They would become mighty by carving out their place in the world—in Israel. These ancients would have found absurd the low regard soldiering commands in today's Judeo-Christian religion. To the contrary, *Israel saw God as a God of war and came to celebrate soldiering as an extension of religion, not as a contradiction to it.* This attitude is amply attested in the following story—one of Bible readers' all-time favorites.

3

David and Goliath

Armed with little more than personal enthusiasm and a slingshot, an inexperienced shepherd boy once took on a towering military Philistine veteran, taunting, "You come with a sword... but I come in the name of the 'Lord of Hosts,' the 'God of the armies of Israel.'" 1 Sam. 17:45 notes and forever immortalizes how well David's moniker described God: the appellation *"Adonoi Sebaot"* ("Lord of Hosts/Armies") appears a further 285 times in the Hebrew Bible.

Writing in *Encyclopaedia Judaica,* Dr. Thorkild Jacobsen, professor of Assyriology at Harvard University, and Dr. Theodore Gaster, of Columbia University, appropriately defined *"Sebaot"* as "a formal militia, marshaled and commanded by God" (Vol. VIII, p. 1044). In David's contest, faith facilitated war and called forth the "hosts," did it not? Mindful of professors Jacobsen and Gaster's contribution, we can deduce that Israel's "God of War" was called upon to secure the battles' objectives, and to protect those precariously engaged in winning them!

Not only did biblical religion prompt individuals *not* to shy away from occasional conflict, it led them to it and through it! This is further demonstrated below.

In 1 Samuel, with God's help, Saul defeated the Ammonites in 11:1-11, much as Jonathan bested the Philistines in 13:5 and 14:31. Tragically, after Saul's initial victory over the Amalekites, in 15:7-9, his depravity got the better of him, leading to his military defeat in chapter 31. David's rise—concurrent with Saul's demise—is well noted in the Text.

The principle that if God were served well, He would serve His people by sustaining their armies was noted many times and was not lost on the ancients. As noted above, in 1 Samuel

Introduction

17, an emboldened and full-of-faith David initially took on Goliath. He then "jumped into the fray" and battled more Philistines in 18:27. He then triumphed over the Amalekites in 27:8 and 30:1-20. In 2 Samuel, with God's indisputable help, David's forces secured a victory over the Jebusites in 5:6-9, over the Philistines again in 5:17-20, over Moab in 8:2, over Zobah in 8:3-4, over Syria in 8:5-6, and Ammon-Rabbah in 11:1 and 12:26-31. David beat Absalom's followers in 18:1-8, Sheba in 20:1-2 and 14-21, and the Philistines again in 21:15-22—all with the "Lord of the Armies."

Though David is the Old Testament's quintessential warrior—and also the archetype of the Hebrew "Messiah"—the Hebrew Bible tells the tales of many other splendid warriors who, at great personal risk, carved out and defended tribal claims in the ancestral homeland—the patriarch Abraham's "Promised Land."

Old Testament authors construe fighting for home and hearth in a positive light, do they not? The New Testament also puts soldiering in a positive light.

It was a centurion—a "battle tested," career, infantry "captain"—in Lk. 7:1-10 who was commended over non-commissioned Judeans. It was a centurion, at Calvary, who first recognized and articulated that Jesus was the "Son of God," in Matt. 27:54. A centurion was the first gentile converted through Peter in Acts 10. A centurion rescued Paul from the Antonia Fortress in Acts 21:32; 22:25. And a centurion treated Paul well during his fateful transport to Rome, in Acts 27:1-44.

It is worth noting that the New Testament commends military field commanders as role models of faith. Writers and early readers of the New Testament would have laughed at the idea that it calls for sheepish and docile responses to adversity and aggression, in the name of Christian virtue.

5

Paul, the New Testament's foremost apostolic commander, comfortably used war pictures to make analogies to the Christian life. In Ephesians 6:10-20, he visualizes battle dress: "Be strong, and put on the whole armor of God"—replete with a "breastplate," "shield," "helmet," and even a "sword." He presupposed that the analogy would strike a positive chord in the minds' eyes of his hearers, and play into the romantic view they held of the Roman infantryman—as was common in the Greco-Roman world. In 1 Tim. 2:3-4, Paul encourages Timothy to "fight the good fight," further underscoring that *soldiering, though indeed unpleasant, was appreciated by biblical writers.*

God's People and War

So as not to seem to glory in war uncritically, let me point out that Jesus' exhortation in Matthew to "not resist an evil person" (5:39), to "give away your cloak" to him who would "take it" (5:40), to somehow "love your enemies" (5:44), and to "be perfect" in the administration of the above (5:48) reminds readers that we ought to prefer being non-combative, and should force Bible readers to look seriously and critically at the legitimacy of war and to wrestle with *if, when,* and *under what conditions* a war could be acceptable, though undesirable.

On the basis of Jesus' words, despite the biblical warrior motifs, those who oppose war and oppose the support of it on religious grounds, appear to have the Christian and moral "high ground," given that their convictions seem closer to the ideals noted in Jesus' words. Religious-minded people like me, who believe in the legitimate use of force (unpleasant though it is), therefore, must give a reasoned accounting for the basis of that belief. And we must substantiate the principles that can guide biblical-minded people in the Godly use of force in times of war and peace.

Introduction

In his *Summa Theologica*, Christian theologian and philosopher Thomas Aquinas leaned on Augustine's "just war" theory, and set the wartime standards for western civilization and Christian culture. After dealing with questions and objections associated with whether it is "always sinful to wage war," Aquinas argued that, "in order for a war to be just, three things are necessary."

First, "the *authority*" of the sovereign by whose command the war is to be waged" must be legitimate. Second, "*a just cause is required*;" namely, that those who are attacked deserve it on account of some fault. Augustine explains: "A just war is wont to be described as one that avenges wrongs, when a nation or state has to be punished for refusing to make amends for the wrongs inflicted by its subjects, or to restore what it has seized unjustly." Third, "it is necessary that they should have a rightful intention, so *that they intend the advancement of good, or the avoidance of evil.*" Hence, Augustine says, "True religion looks upon as peaceful those wars that are waged not for motives of aggrandizement, or cruelty, but with the object of securing peace, of punishing evil-doers, and of uplifting the good." Augustine clarifies: "We do not seek peace in order to be at war, but *we go to war that we may have peace.*"

This line of reasoning has helped Christian power brokers utilize force without incurring undue pangs of conscience. Even so, and for the following reasons, many Christians have trouble coming to terms with the unpleasant legitimacy of employing military options.

Unlike Old Testament Judaism, New Testament Christianity promises no earthly "promised land" for Believers during the Church Age. The Gospel holds out the promise of a future reward for the righteous, true—but, somewhere else; the

7

ultimate reward is in a mansion prepared in Heaven (Jn. 14:2; Php. 3:20-21). Contrary to Old Testament orientations and Jewish expectations, Jesus explicitly noted that His Kingdom was *"not* of this earth" and that He was thus *not* interested in mobilizing Believers to literally fight for it (Jn. 18:36). Thus, we see two trains of thought: one in the Old Testament for Jews, and another in the New Testament for Jesus' followers.

Is Jesus saying that Christians cannot bear arms to defend the interests of their earthly concerns? No. To exist in the real world, Christians cannot skirt life's pressing conflicts. Because Christians have citizenship in two distinct domains—one in the present *Earthly* and another in a coming *Heavenly* realm—Believers had to develop moral criteria to guide their bearing of arms: (1) legitimate state "authority," (2) a defensive and "just cause" and (3) a "rightful intention."

So much for Christians; what of the Jews? If the biblical story is read literally, then, in no uncertain terms, Jews have legitimate "authority" to wage a campaign to secure their biblically sanctioned "Promised Land," not to mention a "just cause" and a proper "intention." *There is no good argument against Jews warring on behalf of Israel in either the Jewish or Christian Bibles.* Hebrews have a legitimate right to fight for the Land, and to fight in defense of it once they are in it—period.

Introducing *Guns & Moses*
Believing all offered so far to be true, let me state clearly that *Guns & Moses* is *not* exclusively about the Jews' right to fight for their ancestral homeland—right though the claim is adjudged by me to be on biblical, legal, and historical grounds. Rather, with that clearly delineated "right" assumed by me as a given, *this book surveys Moses' writings to consider what he says about*

Introduction

the Israelites' use of "might" in the Land, and not just the application of their *"right"* to the Land.

I examined Mosaic literature and asked, *What do these stories and teachings have to say about the way resident Israelites are to deal with non-Israelites, both within and around the Land?* It's about the use of "might," and not just "right." This shifts the book's emphasis away from simply proving that Israel is the Jewish homeland (important as that is), to what God told Moses about *how Jews—and all God's people by association— should use power within their spheres of influence.*

If not in my lifetime, certainly in my teenage children's, I expect the tensions associated with the present Islamic expansion on the once-Christian European continent to come to a head and force a painful response, as Europeans wrestle with questions related to who they are and what they want to be. Will Europeans surrender country after country, and give up the continent outright? Is there even time for them to resist? Are they capable? If Europe manages somehow not to slide into the Islamic fold—as has all of northern Africa, along with many parts of Asia—how will European countries keep alive the vestiges of Christian memory and culture among them, and successfully live with Muslims beside them? These questions are coming. Indeed, they are already here.

What of Islam in America? Islam's rapid growth continues unabated in the States, but seems more a curiosity than a crisis, at the present. As Muslims take government seats—at the city, county, state, and federal levels—and exercise more leverage over our young through our religion-abandoning, secular school systems, should good Americans sit back and give over this country in the name of democracy? I think not! But, how can America exist as a decidedly Judeo-Christian nation and still extend

9

liberties to Muslims dwelling among us? If we don't answer these questions, our children will surely have to.

Might the past have some answers? I think so. This book teases out the laws and stories set down by Moses, which I think are useful in addressing these concerns.

Guns & Moses:
Peace and Power in the Pentateuch

In *Guns & Moses,* I am primarily interested in unpacking the ethical principles discerned in Moses' writings, and pressing them upon my readers' minds. While the ethical principles easily apply to the ongoing Arab-Israeli conflict and to what I anticipate as the impending Arab-European clash, this book's lessons also apply to other situations and can assist a variety of people who employ power—e.g., police officers, judges, politicians, soldiers, employers, parents, etc.—to do so more prudently. The implications abound.

Believing, as I do, that our culture's government, military, criminal justice systems, family systems, educational systems, and value systems were once unapologetically influenced by Judeo-Christian values rooted in biblical literature—derived from the church and synagogue's Bible—*I offer to assist those interested in looking at peace and power, by directly, explicitly, and systematically reintroducing readers to the biblical stories, virtues, and values that initially informed Israel's and our culture's code of conduct, and factored into the way we deal with those who deviate from it.* There is a need for this, I feel—for a variety of reasons.

Years ago, as a graduate student at Southern Methodist University, I took an "invitation only" course entitled "Ethics and Law," a special program offered to select third year law students and third year seminarians. The synergy between the

Introduction

soon-to-be lawyers and pastors was interesting, as was the discovery that *minimal attention was typically given to the ethical training of those who wield social power.* I hope that a book on Moses will prove helpful for those seeking to define and refine their inner constitutions, and will contribute to their personal and professional capability.

Moses exists in our modern consciousness because of his literary contribution, preserved in a collection of biblical books called the Pentateuch—the "Five Books of Moses." There, in the collection's second book, "Exodus," Moses entered the drama, personally, and secured a great deliverance for the Hebrews, professionally, after he went to Pharaoh and insisted, "Let my people go!"—possibly Moses' most famous utterance, though not his first one.

Moses' first lines are noted in Exodus 2:13. There, according to the Text, "he beheld two Hebrew men fighting, and he said to the one who did the wrong, 'Why are you striking your companion?'" Moses is first heard dealing with *civil unrest*—an assault, specifically. Three verses later, in verses 16-17, Moses went on to use physical "force" to protect some unknown women when he saw some shepherd boys "drive away" some girls from a watering hole where the girls had first watering rights. In response, Moses says he "stood up and helped them," thereby securing justice and order. Paul's New Testament historian and interpreter, Luke, commented on Moses' actions saying: "...seeing one of them suffer wrong, he defended and avenged him who was oppressed" (Acts 7:24). Moses reminds me of a cop—and I really love cops! What a guy! I love telling his story.

Given biblical religion's tragic marginalization in the modern, secular economy, I realize that a book extolling such biblical virtue will not go uncontested. Biblical cares and biblical prayers seem deliberately, systematically, and unfairly banished from the "public square" today. Jews are marginalized and Christianity has long been disparaged in our public schools where our young are nurtured. Removing icons that focus on the "Ten Commandments" from some of our courts further trivializes the religious voices and presence that underpin our country's foundation. This is a tragic mistake! I believe that individuals interested in exposing themselves to biblical literature and concepts, for whatever reason(s), will be more successful personally and professionally, aided by the transforming power inherent in God's Word, the Bible. It is my prayer that Its power, with God's help, will shine through my humble efforts in a work of this sort.

Conclusion

In *Guns & Moses*, I intentionally speak *both* as a theologian and as a police officer. I am a proud graduate of the North Texas Regional Police Academy, and I keep an active reserve commission in a patrol division just outside Dallas, Texas. I am honestly proud to be a "cop," and see this activity as one of my life's greatest and most satisfying accomplishments. I have some experience teaching college as a Criminal Justice instructor, as well, and am certified as a Field Training Officer of police and as an Instructor of Police Sciences.

I studied at the Moody Bible Institute in Chicago and was graduated from the theological seminary at Southern Methodist University in Dallas, Texas, where I earned a master's degree and doctorate in theology and ministry. I served as a Bible college professor, both at Christ for the Nations Institute in Dallas, Texas (where I have taught since 1989), and as an adjunct professor at Grace School of Ministry in Houston, Texas. I have also served pastorates for many years. My work appears in *Kairos Journal*, where I, with others, take on issues effecting the erosion of Judeo-Christian virtues in Western

Introduction

culture. In the late spring of 2006, I was asked to walk in the footsteps of Zola Levitt, the greatest and best-known Messianic Jewish communicator of our times. As principal theologian and spokesman for Zola Levitt Ministries I write articles and books and speak to untold millions through our weekly, syndicated television program, "Zola Levitt Presents." With the world focused on Middle Eastern events in and around Israel, I thought this would be a good time to release this particular book, to offer a biblical lens through which to examine police actions in general and Israel's and our own in particular.

As I close, let me express gratitude to Pastor Lee and Mrs. Oh, along with other staff at the theological seminary located at the "Lydia Sisters Mission" in Seoul, Korea. Their invitation to visit and teach a mini-course on the Pentateuch in early 2005 afforded me the opportunity to congeal the thoughts for this book. I'd kicked the material around for years while patrolling in a squad car, working as a cop. Work begun in my mind was committed to writing in Korea, and from there came to term through my association with Zola Levitt Ministries, to which I am, indeed, indebted. To learn more about my ministry, check out www.levitt.com.

Thanks, as always, to my dear wife, Patty, who is forever supportive of me in my various adventures and endeavors, and without whose cooperation this book would not have been possible. That I personally enjoy the support of my two fine sons—Jacob and Zachary—is forever a source of great joy, as well.

Jeffrey L. Seif

March 2007
Dallas, Texas

I

Genesis

Introduction

Moses' fascinating writings have long been misconstrued by non-Jewish churchmen, who often relegate them to the backwaters of biblical study. Perceived as an archaic collection of dry, "legalistic" rules, as an antiquated compendium of anti-spiritual, Jewish "laws," the Pentateuch (meaning the "five books" of Moses) has historically been ignored and disparaged by Christians, depriving many individuals of its benefits, which would otherwise be theirs for the gleaning. *Guns & Moses*, I hope, will correct this pervasive misunderstanding and offer some biblical medicine for modern life's assorted hurts.

Genesis is written in narrative form and has no particularly dry or legislative verbiage to note. Originally known in Hebrew as *Sepher Maaseh Bereshith*, meaning the "Book of Creation," Genesis starts with the beginnings of our cosmos, our planet, and the myriad species who call it home. From the planet's rich soil, *homo sapiens* (literally, "wise man") emerged as the crown of God's creation, creatures made "in God's [very] image."

Shortly thereafter, something went wrong. Genesis places the humans in paradise, and tells how the first man and a woman were bested therein by their greedy impulses. The first couple was summarily evicted from their garden paradise. Sin made its entrance onto the stage of the human drama by coming to Adam and Eve and through them to the rest of creation. Their children and grandchildren went from bad to worse. Disgusted by it all, God destroyed humankind, save Noah. With him, Genesis says, the Lord started afresh after the flood. Still, things went from bad to worse, to worst yet.

Genesis gives a clear picture of the widespread civil and criminal problems inherent in primitive man's breast and world. The people of Israel, as we shall see, were called forth with a Divine mandate to bring about the diseased Earth's redemption. Genesis was that priestly nation-state's ethics primer—its schoolmaster. As such, Genesis instructs directly and descriptively regarding a host of social and spiritual matters that confront and affect humankind. Young Israelites were to "cut their teeth" on Genesis—and on the rest of the Pentateuch; through their exposure to its stories and principles, they were to be transformed into the people of God, and become a light to the sin-soaked, darkened world they inhabited. But, first, the Israelites needed enlightenment to master the darker side of their own sin-soaked natures and confused inner worlds. With Scripture lighting their way, they were to shine as lights in the broader culture. We will see God's plan emerge as we unpack some of Genesis' particulars and shed light on issues relevant to our own modern world.

Exposition of Genesis

In Genesis 1:1-6:8, Moses offers a brief narration of the origin of our planet and the various, God-made species that call it home.

In chapters 1 and 2, God created the material world out of cosmic nothingness and disorder, and then placed humankind upon it with the mandate to help "order" and "establish" the planet (1:28-30). Debates rage about whether the six days of creation should be taken literally or symbolically. Irrespective of how one answers, and beyond debate, God is represented as miraculously creating the planet, endorsing it as "good," supernaturally manufacturing humankind, and giving us the mandate to manage it properly.

Adam and Eve enjoyed felicity for a season in their enclosed paradise. Their fortunes changed immediately and dramatically, however—and ours with theirs, by association. Their "good life," we're told, was interrupted by sin's uninvited entrance into their paradise (3:1-24), through their unbridled acquisitiveness. They had everything but one thing—a forbidden fruit—and they let themselves be talked into just having to have it. Their greedy, acquisitive natures got the better of them, and of us by extension.

The rest is history.

Genesis observes trouble within the human community immediately after creation when Adam and Eve did intentionally and knowingly, and without the owner's effective consent, appropriate another's property—a forbidden fruit, in this particular case (2:8, 16-17; 3:1-8). Alas, a "theft" immediately after creation. When questioned about the misdeed, neither Adam nor Eve accepted personal responsibility for the malefaction (3:9-24). The situation was not successfully remedied. God, as a result, had the two summarily removed from the Garden, and the first couple lost the privileges and liberties associated with living therein.

What might the ancients have learned from this? Possibly, that living in peace and security with God's blessings is predicated upon humans' compliance with others' property rights; that humans will lose dwelling privileges in their land if they don't act in a civilized manner. Adrift now, Adam and Eve were forced to renegotiate a new life for themselves elsewhere, ejected from the paradise that they once called home. Genesis swiftly informs readers that something went horribly wrong with *homo sapiens*: the human "wise man" showed himself to be a fool.

Themes evident in the biblical narrative's miserable opening include: (1) God's interest in the emergence of order out of human chaos and disorder, (2) Man's disorderly and flagrant refusal to acknowledge the lawful property rights of others, and, (3) the perennial tensions inherent in the human breast. The battle between need and greed, and between virtue and vice is shown early on by Adam and Eve's wrestling with their inflamed desires and eventual succumbing to their acquisitive natures.

If that weren't bad enough, readers further discover that matters spiraled downward, going from bad to worse through the rest of the narrative—through the entire Bible, in fact. While there's Good News coming, we must be patient before getting to it: Bible readers are directed to more bad news, first.

Genesis

Following immediately on the heels of the Eden property crime, in 4:1-16 Israel's "lawgiver" Moses notes that the criminal and capital offense of assault and murder—domestic and family violence, particularly—was the first recorded activity of the race's natural born children, the offspring of the apparently then-jaded "human" species.

The human race showed its capacity to be inhumane right from the start.

Culpable as his father Adam was, a jealous Cain, says Moses, did intentionally and knowingly murder his brother Abel (4:1-10), with the result that Cain—himself just a generation removed from Adam—was sentenced to be a "fugitive and vagabond on the earth" (v. 14). As with Adam, he was thus farther removed from civilization and from the initial paradise that was humankind's intended home—the now-forgotten place called "Eden."

Marriage
Uncivilized as Cain apparently was, Moses informs us that Cain's lusty offspring, Lamech, proceeded to "take two wives for himself" (v. 19)—contrary to the preferred scenario of "one man, one woman"—and that he boasted of another offense to civilized behavior: "I have killed a man for wounding me" (v. 23).

In 2:24, Genesis depicts a man "leaving his father and his mother to be joined to his wife"—singular—worth noting is the preference for monogamy. The Text does not legitimize leaving father and more to be joined to "wives"—plural. No matter, man's acquisitive nature led him to this and other forms of defilement. In but the first few chapters of biblical text we observe *crimes of theft, perjury, murder, and adultery!* Then, chapter 6 introduces readers to still more forms of

19

defilement and human degradation related to sexual promiscuity and violence.

"It came to pass," says Moses, "when men began to multiply on the face of the earth, and daughters were born to them," that men "took to themselves daughters of men that were beautiful... all whom they chose" (6:1-2). So provoked was God by this unbridled greed leading to mankind's display of social and sexual indiscretion, that God regretted "that He had made man" (vv. 6-7). A sobering summary of the creation account follows: "The earth was *corrupt* before God, and the earth was *filled with violence*" (v. 11). Not a good commentary, to be sure.

One needn't be a cop, a criminal justice professor, a lawyer, or a judge to see where things were headed. The crimes of theft, assault/family violence, murder, sexual offenses, and more appear in the Bible's opening statements. Were a professionally trained patrol officer or district attorney to examine society in early Genesis with a "penal code" in hand (i.e., the code noting assorted crimes and punishments), the investigator would easily discover specific facts that would lead reasonable persons to believe "beyond reasonable doubt," that particular crimes had been committed, and that particular persons were clearly responsible for those crimes.

Genesis describes one crime scene after another!

The limited story of humankind's origin, in fact, places more emphasis on the race's criminal *regress* than it does its creation and *progress*. God created order out of chaos; tragically, however, disorder became the "order of the day," with the result that humankind's moral compass was clouded over—as it remains to this day, in many respects.

Genesis

Though God had established a law of sorts and planted a guidance mechanism in humanity's conscience, lawlessness was rampant: individuals denied their inner witness; humans wrongfully placed a premium on vice over virtue, and disregarded their innate moral inclinations. With records of thefts, assaults, murders, drunken and disorderly conduct, and unbridled sexual appetites the planet was on a fast track toward destruction—right from the start.

And God destroyed it!

Noah and the Flood

Much as a judge allows a victim's family members to watch a condemned perpetrator's execution from a designated gallery, in 6:9-11:32 Moses gives readers a window into the destruction that was God's judgment upon His recalcitrant creation—our jaded human race. Bible readers are apprised of the flood narrative. A variety of sources tell of the flood—ancient world literature outside biblical influence, and cultures outside the ancient world—lending credence to the biblical account. Chapter 6 tells how the floodwaters decimated the planet; Chapter 8 tells us how they benignly receded. Save for "righteous" Noah and his family in the ark, none survived.

After the waters receded, Moses promptly notes that Noah had a drinking problem—one that left him somewhat vulnerable.

Family dysfunction, which often accompanies drunkenness—then, as now—surfaced immediately after the flood, in 9:18-27. Though Noah could survive the flood as a reward for righteousness, the Earth's most-hopeful citizen (Noah) is seen drowning in his own liquor, found in a drunken stupor, and then exploited by the voyeuristic impulses of his own undisciplined son.

21

Guns & Moses

All this happened—and we're only about fifteen minutes into the Bible's reading, starting in Genesis 1:1. We have a problem, do we not? Bible readers are led to believe that we do.

If one assumes that God inspired the writing of the Scriptures—the operative assumption of this author—then it's apparent that something has gone horribly wrong with God's creation and there seems to be no remedy in sight. At least not yet.

Tower of Babel

After noting individuals' acts of impropriety, and subsequently noting the nations descended from Noah in chapter 10, Moses tells us that the jaded human race was power-hungry, proud (11:4, 6), and bent on celebrating its prowess and conquest by cooperating in building a tower—one that would somehow get them to the heavens (v. 4). In 11:1-9, Moses relates the story of the "Tower of Babel" and notes the halting of the bold project. We're told that, at Babel, God intentionally caused the emboldened people to lose the ability to speak a common language (vv. 7, 9). Unable to communicate, they were forced to give up the project—thus the origin of the term "babble." As for constructing a passageway to Heaven, readers learn that it will take more than just a carpenter to get there.

Abraham

Against the backdrop of the abandoned, man-initiated, worldwide religious project (v. 8), the prospect of one people accomplishing a significant work for humanity and for God is reintroduced. In 11:10-32, Moses offers more genealogical data, and sets the stage for the emergence of one particular person. Moses tells us that, through Abraham, a people will emerge from the vitiated race. This people will eventually offer a means for peace on Earth and goodwill toward men, and will introduce a real highway to Heaven.

Genesis

Before we leave the biblical record of early civilization behind and attend to God's program for biblical betterment by establishing law and order through Abraham and his progeny, we should consider what is, perhaps, the most salient observation that emerges from our cursory glance at mankind's primeval history.

Clearly, in no uncertain terms, the historical and theological record delivered to us by Israel's lawgiver, Moses, shows how *debased, lawless, and uncivilized the world really was*—and still is, left unbridled by conscience and biblical virtue. Obviously, the human community was in trouble from the start. Abraham's contribution to mankind assumed prophetic significance with the promise that he would be the progenitor of a "great nation," one that would eventually become noteworthy through a host of contributions to human betterment (12:1-3).

Interestingly, Moses anticipated that, through Abraham, "*all* the families of the earth will [eventually] be blessed." That the emphasis is *not* exclusive to Hebrews alone, but to "*all*" people, is important. Abraham is pictured as a fountainhead for the eventual outpouring of God's blessing and grace to all.

Exactly how would this be fulfilled? How would "all" humankind be assisted through Abraham? At the start we're told that a large measure of benefit would come through a sense of law and order that would come forth through Abraham's children.

Speaking of, and to, some of those Jewish offspring centuries later, Isaiah exhorted his Jewish hearers, saying, "Look to Abraham your father" (Isa. 51:2a). Listen to what God said then: for a "*Law will proceed from Me*, and I will make My *justice* rest as a light *to the nations*" (italics mine; Isa. 51:4). The psalmist in 99:4 agrees: "You have established *equity*; you have *executed justice* and *righteousness* in Jacob." This particular religious language harkens to the premium that biblical writers placed on virtue and justice for all, moral attributes said to have come uniquely through Abraham's offspring—from whom came biblical revelation and God Himself. At issue through Abraham is a means for the emergence of order out of the world's chaos.

The Torah, the five books of Moses, speaks to a sickened world, one wracked by social unrest and widespread abuse. In this study we will see the Torah's incomparable contribution to righteous jurisprudence, as well as the belief that the lack of virtue in human affairs, through violations of personal and property rights and other affronts to human dignity and justice, is a religious, and not merely a social, offense.

Beginning with the "call" of Abraham, in chapters 12 -17, Moses' readers look through a window into the darkened world made a little brighter by Abraham's arrival in it; for, with him comes the Bible's first glimpse of needed, positive, and refreshing "good news" for planet Earth.

Beginning with the "covenant," (12:1-3), God walked through the "ups and downs" of the still-human experience of His newly appointed salvation-bringer, Abraham. In 12:10-14:24, Abraham's faith was tested. Though he failed the first test miserably by temporarily abandoning his wife (vv.10-20; and again in 20:1-18), he fixed his problem(s) and fared better thereafter.

Personal difficulties and imperfections notwithstanding, in 14:1-17, Abraham's religious virtue rose above his human foibles when he courageously "took on" a sizable war party

Genesis

on a relative's behalf. His nephew, Lot, was overrun and, with his possessions and family, was taken off as spoils of war. Upon learning of this, Abraham marshaled his resources, went after the bellicose party, defeated them, rescued Lot, and returned the richer for it. That he subsequently tithed some of his "spoils of war" to a priest named Melchizedek, serves as a testimony to a cultivated religious virtue (vv. 18-20)—one readers would do well to imitate.

In the wake of this defeat over the confederacy of Mesopotamian kings (yesterday's Mesopotamia being the region occupied by modern Iraq, and parts of Syria, Turkey, and Iran), Genesis notes in chapter 14 and 15:1 that God affirmed Abraham saying, "Do not be afraid, Abram, I am your shield." Amidst the turbulence of trying times, God promised to help Abraham make his way into the future, and preserve his posterity to accomplish their destiny—and God's by association. Surely, it has as much relevance today in modernity as it had yesterday in antiquity, when Abraham fought the same regional powers bent on his demise.

In response to assurance that God would be with him, a seemingly ungrateful Abraham took issue with the Lord for His leaving him childless through the years (15:2-21). God patiently bore with the frustrated fellow, led him outside to "look at the stars" and reassured him that his "descendants would be as the stars of Heaven" and "the sand of the seashore" (15:5-6).

Ishmael
The promise seemed slow in coming, however. Wanting to be ever helpful, and likely embarrassed at her inability to provide an heir, Abraham's wife, Sarah, concocted a scheme to remedy the frustrating situation: "Go into my maid; perhaps I shall obtain children by her," she told Abraham. Trying to be the

faithful and compliant husband as he apparently now was, Abram went along with the scheme; in chapter 16, he sort of married Sarah's Egyptian handmaiden Hagar, and sired Ishmael—who is said to have become the progenitor of the Arab peoples.

Prophetically, the Text says of Ishmael—and of his offspring: he shall be the father of a great people (21:13); and, "He shall be a wild man; and his hand shall be against every man; and every man's hand against him; And he shall dwell in the presence of all his brethren" (16:12). Because the whole world was untamed and "wild" at the time, and wars flared up continually, then as now, one wonders what is meant by this prophecy. Could it be that by being consigned to live beyond the biblical land and biblical influence, this son of Abraham would not be blessed by the benefits associated with the Mosaic economy? In saying "he shall dwell in the presence of his brethren," could it mean that he will be "close to" but still "disconnected from"? So it would seem.

Islam understands Arab people to be descended from Ishmael, and Arabs constitute a great mass of people, blessed by massive amounts of the Earth's energy resources—oil and gas. One can't miss the correlation of tensions between Ishmael and his brothers as prophesied in Genesis, and the daily news reports that seem to prove the fulfillment of this ancient promise.

After stressing the importance of circumcision as a "sign of the covenant" (17:9-14), the Lord told Abraham that He would visit Sarah and give her the long-promised son (v. 16). Abraham responded, saying, "Oh, that Ishmael might live before You!" in verse 18. But God said, "No, Sarah your wife shall bear you a son, and you shall call his name Isaac; I will establish my covenant with him, and with his descendants after him" (v. 19). Upon overhearing this, Sarah laughed.

After promising that Ishmael would "be fruitful" and become a "great nation," too (v. 20), God affirmed in verse 21 that He meant Isaac to inherit the promises named in 12:2-3: "But My covenant I will establish with Isaac, whom Sarah shall bear to you." Scripture is emphatic, is it not?

Abraham's advocating for Ishmael holds a lesson for us. Even while granting Israel's right to exist as a Jewish homeland, Bible readers should respect the promise God made to Ishmael.

Tensions associated with the Hebrews' and Arabs' relationship to Abraham's land continues into the present generation. Troubling though this is, the unyielding angst testifies to the veracity of Scripture, proving that the ancient story has relevance to the modern world.

Putting the reasonably happy predictions of Sarah's promised child aside for the moment, the placid patriarchal narrative is interrupted by word of sexually-related social offenses infecting a sector of the broader culture.

Sodom and Gomorrah

After giving the rules of circumcision (whereby the foreskin of a covenant male's penis was to be marked) Genesis 18:1-15 tells us that messengers visited Abraham bringing word of licentious Sodom's inevitable annihilation—judgment for its rank perfidy. (We get the word "sodomy" from this story.) Abraham's religious intercession failed to assuage the Divine retribution that was soon visited upon the sexually perverted culture (vv. 16-33). The juxtaposition of circumcision as a "sign of the covenant" and the story of sexual perversion in Sodom lends credence to the proposition that circumcision itself tacitly suggests that being part of God's covenant people entails disciplined sexual practice. Instead of it simply being a ritual, circumcision also serves as this reminder: that testosterone-driven impulses should be tempered by the demands of the covenant, a covenant not just written in stone, but written in skin.

Lot

The angelic messengers left Abraham and made their way to Sodom, where they took up temporary residence with Lot, in 19:1-28. Evidence of Sodom's horrendous debauchery is seen immediately. The messengers themselves faced the prospects of being sexually assaulted and exploited at the hands of a howling mob of lusty homosexuals (19:5).

Lawless men surrounded the house where the gentle messengers bedded down for the night, and were hell bent on molesting them (19:1-4). The anxious mob pressed Lot to turn over his guests, so that the men might "lie with them carnally," in verse 5. This is an explicit reference to homosexual sex—homosexual "gang rape," in this case. So overrun were these men by their misguided sexual appetites, Lot and the messengers were saved only by Divine intervention (v. 11).

Being forewarned of the coming judgment, Lot made haste to depart, taking with him whomever he could. Tragically and contrary to command, his wife turned back as "the Lord rained brimstone and fire on Sodom and Gomorrah" (v. 24) and she met her untimely end as a pillar of salt.

But, who could blame her for looking back? Leaving behind daughters and grandchildren no doubt fired her natural, maternal instincts and prompted her to "look back" as the heavens thundered destruction upon the city, and upon her family members still living there. That she shared their fate

Genesis

serves as a reminder that collateral damage always accompanies sexual indiscretion.

Lot's dwelling in Sodom and in close proximity to such rank wickedness proved his undoing, though he did not partake in the illicit practices himself. Fleeing for his life, and with a couple of single daughters in tow (for whom he now had no dowry), the once powerful and wealthy Lot ended his days living as an impoverished vagabond, hopelessly dwelling with his beautiful, unmarried daughters in a cold cavern. Though Abraham had rescued him previously and restored his fortunes to him (Gen. 14), in this case he was not rescued, but finished his days ingloriously.

Moses depicts Lot as a shell of a man living as a drunken bum, residing in the cave to which he escaped after the raging inferno destroyed all of the wealth that he had accumulated. Marooned with him, his lovely daughters had no prospects for successfully finding love and marriage. As a result, Gen. 19: 30-38 tells us how they put their father in an inebriated state, lay with him, and finally bore children through their incestuous contact with him. One son was called "Moab," from whom the world got the Moabites (v. 37); the other was "Ben-Ammi," from whom the Ammonites descended (v. 38).

The primeval Genesis narrative notes the havoc that bad choices caused for Adam, Eve, Cain, Lamech, Noah, Ham, those at Babel, and Lot. Abraham's story plays out against the backdrop of a lawless and condemned world, depicted as "going from bad to worse." Moses describes wayward humans living out miserable lives in a miserable and lawless world. Discontented folk are seen wallowing and drowning in their own shame and vomit. Tragically, this is what became of God's special creation and life on God's good Earth! From this quandary, Abraham is called forth and vouchsafed a "promised land," as other people round about are shown as possessing a penchant for wickedness.

In sum, the first twenty chapters of Holy Writ serve up stories of a world wracked by assaults, sexual assaults/rapes, cases of assault/family violence, thefts, murders, and the like. Though the situation deteriorated "from bad to worse," God divulges His plan to show a better "way" through a group of chosen people: through Abraham, Isaac, and Jacob—with an aside dedicated to Abraham's son Ishmael.

Isaac

Chapter 21 returns to Abraham's story and tells us that following Isaac's birth Abraham was "tested" to ascertain whether he'd willingly give up the long-promised lad were God to command it (22:1-19). Dutifully, Abraham took his son to Mount Moriah to offer him as a "sacrifice." Happily for both, it was only a test—and an odd one at that.

Benefits accrue to those who follow God's sometimes hard-to-comprehend instructions, even when they conflict with natural base impulses (as with there seeming to be no good reason to take Isaac's life). Taming base impulses and following instructions is a necessary prerequisite for being civil and, thus, participating in civilization.

Abraham, compliant with mandates—even ones hard to follow—passed God's test. Speaking of "passing," but in another context altogether, Moses goes on to tell of Sarah's "passing," by noting her death and burial in 23:1-20. This sad story is immediately followed by the need to provide a new "lady of the house"—a special bride for the miracle-child who carried the "promise" of humankind's hope and restoration: Isaac (24:1-67).

Genesis

Rebekah

Given the manifold examples of man's weaknesses, one wonders: Where in the world do you go to find a virtuous woman? An elderly Abraham gave his chief steward (15:2) the task in 24:1-9. Off he went in 24:10 to find a literal answer to the question of how to find a worthy wife for the special boy of his master's old age.

Wanting a "good woman," and not just a "good looking" one (for looks can be deceiving), the prudent servant ventured into what is probably Iraq today, to the town of Nahor, and asked the Lord to bring a woman to him, for Isaac. Of particular interest was finding a Semitic relative who would meet particular *character-related criteria*. The discerning steward devised a unique sign for God to make His choice known.

She would not only have to be attractive, but she would have to be *kindly disposed toward strangers*—demonstrated by her willingness to assist him on the road (24:10-28), and she would have to be *kindly disposed toward animals* (vv. 14 and 20-22), an interesting proclivity, to be sure. At a well in Nahor, a young Semitic woman gave water to the tired man from Israel and also to his camels.

Would that such virtue abounded among Abraham's offspring in and around the Middle East today! Being kindly disposed toward others seems lacking in the region. Islam now dominates and "outsiders" (non-Muslims) are threatened and intimidated into subservience. While Islamic rhetoric calls for "love" and "brotherhood," reality paints a different picture. Bombastic, savage, and cruel acts are perpetuated in the name of religion, with no objections raised. God hasten the day when the winds of change blow, when more good-natured Rebekahs will appear in the Middle East.

31

Guns & Moses

Abuse and Animals

It is worth noting that criminal justice studies prove what readers of this particular account have known all along: *there is a correlation between good character and kindness to animals.* One particular study of criminal pathology notes that almost all prison inmates "doing time" for violent crimes had childhood histories of abusing animals. Today, peace officers are trained to look for signs of cruelty to animals when responding to "calls for service" at residences; for animal abuse is a marker pointing to crimes against people, given the extremely strong correlation between cruelty to animals and cruelty to humans. Judeo-Christian cultures have "humane societies" where we treat our animals much better than some other cultures treat their humans. We do this because we possess a superior virtue, one founded on a set of better principles—the Scriptures. At day's end, Judeo-Christian ethics, rooted in Judeo-Christian faith and literature, yield a better product, a better culture.

Esau and Jacob

With Isaac married, Moses tells of Abraham's death in 25:1-10. As the story of the clan unfolds in 25:19-28:9, Isaac and Rebekah gave birth to twins: Esau and Jacob (25:19-34). Then sadly, like Abraham before him, Isaac demonstrated lackluster resolve to lay claim to his marriage. In chapter 26, much as with Abraham in 12:10-20 and again in 20:1-18, Isaac, mindful of his lawless environment, was afraid that the men of Gerar would note his attractive wife and kill him to secure her for themselves. Wanting to survive, he passed off his wife as his "sister" in verse 7—a story already repeated too many times in the narrative. He later "came clean" and she was returned to him, with the annoyed ruler's blessing.

That God graciously bore Isaac's foibles seems apparent. That the sins of the fathers are sometimes visited upon succeeding generations seems apparent as well: in this case, Isaac sinned in much the same way as his father—not a pleasant observation.

Moses then contrasts individuals' marriage choices, informing us that Esau had grown up and married two Hittite women from the area, Judith and Basemath; both were deemed "a grief of mind to Isaac and Rebekah" (26:34). That biblical personalities have such tendencies is significant, and more will be said of this later in Exodus and Numbers.

In chapter 27, Jacob secured the "birthright" and "blessing of Abraham" from Isaac, his father, by stealth and then, at his mother's behest, went off to Padan-Aram to find a wife for himself. Moses again informs that Rebekah was sorely distressed by her eldest son Esau's poor marriage choices, in 27:46. She was displeased because he married locals outside the clan. Marrying well was of extreme importance in Genesis and failure to do so was deemed to be extremely problematic. In this case, it seems that "marrying well" entailed looking beyond the local resource pool of available partners, for a woman armed with compatible religious and social dispositions. Were these characteristics lacking in Esau's wives, or did their mother-in-law reject them on racial grounds?

Leah and Rachel

Irrespective, the narrative moves along focusing on Jacob's journey to Padan-Aram (modern Syria), recounted in 28:10-22. In chapter 29, he encountered Rachel—and then her stealthy father, Laban. Jacob wound up marrying into this dishonest and storm-tossed family, and was disconcerted by the attendant dysfunction.

After working for Laban for seven years to secure Rachel's hand in marriage, Jacob wound up first marrying her sister, Leah, as a result of Laban's manipulations, a tendency that extended to his business affairs, too. Even more acquisitions of women follow in 30:1-13. A spirited "catfight" ensued after the marriages, fueled by jealousy associated with Rachel's inability to have children, and Leah's ability to bear them with relative ease. Finally, after producing nearly a dozen sons, in 30:25-32:3, Jacob opted to extricate himself from his father-in-law and set his sights south by southwest, and toward his God-given ancestral home in Israel, with his large family in tow, in 32:4-36:43.

That the land of Israel was given to Jacob and his offspring is explicitly stated in the literature. But his brother Esau had other thoughts and now Jacob had to contend with him. Given Esau's violent nature, coupled with Jacob having left him previously on less-than-desirable terms, in 32:4-33:10, Jacob devised a strategy to "win him over." Jacob had a plethora of gifts presented to Esau, hoping to assuage his anger—at least temporarily. Happily, it worked. Jacob made peace with Esau when he returned, and settled back in the region with tense assurances.

Dinah – Concessions and Peace
Jacob's relative calm was short-lived, however. A young man in a neighboring Hittite town took an apparent liking to Jacob's attractive, only daughter, Dinah. Moses informs us, "he took her and lay with her, and violated her" (34:2)—what moderns would call consensual "fornication" at best, "rape" at worst. Attracted to her and earnestly wanting to do right by her (vv. 3-4), he propositioned to take her permanently as a wife—what was apparently a noble attempt to ameliorate the lusty impropriety. While sex outside of marriage is never the preferred scenario, the young man wanted to do right by her, a credit to his account.

Genesis

Though not the preferred scenario for Israelites, Esau married neighboring Hittite women. So, perhaps with the precedent already established, Jacob seemed willing to agree to Dinah's marriage—and even seemed to prefer the peace it promised. But his wishes did not prevail. His sons (Dinah's brothers), by contrast, would have none of it! With brazen disregard for their father's wishes, and with intrepid boldness, in 34:13-29 they took matters into their own hands. Moses tells how they ambushed the Hittite town and killed the Hittite residents, further invoking their father's ire (vv. 30-31).

Tensions between the Hebrews and the locals seem to abound in the literature right on down to the present. Jacob's willingness to come to terms with the Hittites seems to bode well: Though wronged, Jacob kept his anger in check, and was inclined to meet their concessions in the interest of peace.

Would that cooler temperaments prevailed in the region, today! If only the Middle East found more men like Jacob and the Hittites! Perpetuating slaughter is not preferred in the biblical testimony. Better to cooperate in the interest of forging peace.

Of course, it did not happen in this case: Jacob's sons mercilessly slaughtered the Hittites. With murder following fast on the heels of the initial sexual indiscretion, Jacob made haste to journey to Bethel where he had a transformative religious experience: God visited him and his destiny was affirmed (35:1-15). Still, life wasn't smooth. His wife Rachel died during childbirth (vv. 16-20). Isaac died shortly thereafter (vv. 27-29). After a rather lengthy telling of Esau's lineage—through Edom (the Edomites of Moses' day, and the Jordanians in our day) in chapter 36, the narrative shifts to social unrest and political intrigue in Jacob's own household (chapters 37-40).

Guns & Moses

Joseph

The story of Joseph, the second-to-youngest son of Jacob shows that Jewish people are not perfect people. Jacob's sons not only betrayed their father's wishes to vent their fury on the Hittites, they also betrayed one of their own—Joseph.

The seventeen-year-old's fall by the hands of jealous brothers who betrayed him to merchants headed to Egypt, is told in chapter 37. This was something of a low point in Judean history, further attested by Moses' telling of Judah's indiscretion with a woman believed by him to be a prostitute, in chapter 38.

The narrative thus contrasts *Judah's wantonness* with *Joseph's sterling virtue*. It notes Joseph's degradation in captivity, but then emphasizes his subsequent rise in Egypt, where he eventually became a powerful regent in the land (chapter 41).

Joseph's providential rise in Egypt should be credited, at a certain level, to the account of Egypt's non-Hebrew leader. That an "outsider"—and a Hebrew one at that—would be recognized and elevated as a regent in Egypt is outstanding.

Joseph's helping the Egyptians provided the means for him to help his own clan back in Canaan. If only the spirit of mutual assistance prevailed in the region, today. All could benefit! As with Joseph, would that more people in the region would be willing to recognize worthy contributions made by others—even Jews."

In any case, present musings and hopes aside, the narrative's point is simple: *Righteous conduct triumphs at day's end*, difficulties with Egyptians (and all people!) notwithstanding. As Joseph's case demonstrates, God blesses those with character and righteous conduct, even if they reside in a world where it is in high demand and short supply.

Genesis

When famine forced Joseph's estranged brothers into Egypt to acquire sustenance, Joseph was in a position to do something. That he wasn't vindictive is significant and indicates how God prefers us to forgive those who do wrongs, as opposed to carrying grudges and waiting in secret for an opportunity to vent the pent-up fury. Joseph saw his brothers and set the stage for an interesting and successful reunion (42:1-47:27). With the family reunited, Moses relates Jacob's blessings to his offspring in 47:28-49:33 and describes Jacob's and Joseph's burials in chapter 50. As Genesis closes, the Israelites dwell securely in Egypt—a situation that would change drastically in the not-too-distant future.

Summary and Lessons Learned

Genesis readers observe that *immediately after the human experience was inaugurated, humankind spiraled out of control with stories of civil unrest and criminal offenses leaping off the pages in the ancient Scriptures, from beginning to end.*

With the passage of time, and against the backdrop of the world's miserable decline, God marked Abraham for a particular "calling" and destiny—*to bring social order out of the prevailing chaos through a religious and morally inclined faith and subsequent "code."*

Though Abraham and his offspring bore the inglorious marks of the condemned human species themselves—their shortcomings are plainly evident in biblical literature—one can still perceive ethical virtues resonating in the patriarchal narratives (compared to the primitive and problematic behaviors of neighboring peoples). These virtues will be articulated more clearly in the Mosaic writings that follow.

Guns & Moses

Genesis shows us strength, with God's promise to go before His people and give them success in life and war. The patriarchal stories commend to us *righteousness, justice, and kindness,* though these are typically overshadowed by their absence in the prevailing culture.

What is Genesis' primary purpose?

Moses gave an account of creation, sin's entrance, and civil conflict. Was he trying to write a college-level biology textbook on the origin of the planet and of the species resident upon it? I think not—though I believe credible information germane to humankind's creation and primeval experience can certainly be gleaned from it. Was he offering a comprehensive telling of the human race's beginnings? The answer is "no" given that the story is not comprehensive at all.

Moses—Israel's illustrious "Lawgiver"—notes that, against the backdrop of criminal offenses, civil unrest, and disorder, a virtue would emerge to ameliorate the decaying situation. Genesis, thus construed, is a pre-history that *sets the stage for the ethical triumph delivered in Exodus,* the giving of the "Law"—itself an instruction book for all people.

Moses wrote his quasi-historical, theological reflections on human origins—dealing with the beginnings of the Hebrew race (though not exclusively) and the beginnings of measured religious ethical instruction in narrative form—originally to service the needs and interests of a ragtag population of freed slaves, a beaten people, themselves just recently rescued from hundreds of years of wretched and oppressive Egyptian bondage.

Genesis

At issue wasn't where the world came from, or even where all of the people of the world came from (Arabs, Europeans, Asians and others), as much as *where the Hebrews came from.*

Genesis told them where they were from and who they were! Genesis reminded an ancient slave people that, though their circumstances through many centuries of Egyptian oppression had not reflected it, they were really descended from a unique race and were, in fact, a "Chosen People." Furthermore, Genesis taught them that they were destined to overcome their adversaries and to help displace the prevailing spiritual darkness and social oppression that characterized life on Earth since the dawn of creation.

Genesis, then, serves as a prelude to the coming Moses-related deliverance and the giving of the "Law" on Sinai, which enables a superior way of life.

II

Exodus

Introduction

Theirs was a world surprisingly similar to our own. In Exodus, Moses bids readers to go back in time to a trying world, one traditionally placed somewhere between the fifteenth and thirteenth centuries B.C. There, Israelites were betrayed by a powerful nation-state, and were sorely oppressed by it.

Several hundred years had passed since Joseph and his brothers enjoyed well-earned benefits at the hand of a Hebrew-friendly Egyptian monarch, kindly disposed toward the Israelites. A new dictator had come to power, and he brought with him a devilish, anti-Hebrew disposition—a decidedly racist inclination, one too often observed in human affairs.

When Moses was born, an official state policy mandated infanticide for newborn Hebrew males—ethnic cleansing, genocide! Whereas, Genesis readers previously read of individuals being victimized by murder, plunder, and theft, *Exodus readers are exposed to advanced forms of social decay.* Exodus differs from Genesis in that defilement is systematized and institutionalized by means of government–sponsored, racist, anti-Hebraism. What were previously random acts of personal aggression and oppression now take form through inhumane systemic expression, with nefarious policies that deliberately reduce human beings to the status of a non-human sub-species. Though the victimized Hebrews were unable to extricate themselves, by themselves, their fortunes were to change with Moses' arrival and meteoric rise.

Exodus is the story of God's deliverance of His people. It tells how He led them to their God-ordained, ancestral homeland, and records His instructions to them on how they were to interact with each other and with outsiders once they became established in that land.

Exposition of Exodus
The Story of Moses
In Exodus 1:1-6:1, Moses describes the abysmal circumstances that preceded the deliverance wrought through him some eighty years after the book opens. Chapter 1 notes how conditions deteriorated following the time of Joseph. In chapter 2 we learn the story of Moses' birth, concealment, and placement in a tiny ark, sent floating down the Nile. His miraculous rescue and rise as a privileged, adopted son in Pharaoh's household follows, with his seemingly tragic decline.

Exodus

Sensitive to the abuses of the underclasses (whom he recognized as his brethren), and frustrated by his inability to alleviate the Hebrews' suffering, a privileged, but vexed, Moses eventually lashed out and slew an Egyptian taskmaster, incurring the wrath of Pharaoh, which forced Moses to flee the realm and what had been his privileged station. Alone and adrift, Moses found himself in a strange new land.

Conventional wisdom says that trials have ways of testing and proving us; and here, giving truth to that maxim, a salient aspect of Moses' unique nature resurfaced.

Though alone in the wilderness, Moses took his character with him. Just after fleeing Egypt, and while resting by a well deep in the Sinai, Moses observed local shepherd boys harassing some shepherd girls. In response, Moses impulsively—and with no thought of his own security or interests—"stood up and helped them" (2:17). The girls promptly notified their father about the cool, new guy in town (v. 19). Personal risk and fatigue notwithstanding, *Moses possessed a sensitive and just disposition*: innate tendencies within his breast fired his energies, prompting him to take up for the weak being pushed around by the strong.

Moses' "police action" is worthy of commentary. We do well to remember that Moses' flight from Egypt was precipitated by his reactive fight with an Egyptian taskmaster, found by him to be senselessly abusing a Hebrew slave. From Moses' perspective, he happened upon a powerful man mistreating someone from the Hebrew underclass—an act that invoked his ire. Here, in much the same manner, and still reeling from his experience and hasty flight from Egypt, Moses intuitively stood up to defend women being mistreated by some more-powerful young men. In both cases, Moses was guided by an innate inclination "to protect and to serve" the oppressed.

Guns & Moses

Moses—Israel's "lawgiver"—operated intellectually from a mindset that valued the needs and interests of oppressed and distressed people. This was Moses; and this was to be Judaism—and then Christianity. It is worth noting the rather sensitive nature of the man who would one day become Israel's chief magistrate—and the world's by extension. While many men's interests diminish as they contemplate the needs of the world that exists beyond their own personal noses, Moses' interests seemingly did not: his vision extended beyond himself, to the weak. Contrary to the prevailing trend, he had a strong social conscience, an unwavering interest in justice and righteousness for *all*, and, as a result, was just the sort of person whom God could use to accomplish something significant—namely, the deliverance of a superior ethic, one that would stand in marked contrast to the barbaric practices of the Egyptians, comfortably situated just over his horizon, and of neighboring Bedouin peoples round about.

After forty years passed, something amazing happened—a thing that would change Moses' fortunes, Israel's fortunes, and the world's. After retreating to the backside of the wilderness for what may have seemed a lifetime, Moses was eventually retrieved by God for God's good purposes through a "burning bush" experience, noted in 3:1-4:17.

After surrendering to the calling (4:18-6:1), Moses' deliverance ministry in Egypt was inaugurated with assorted signs and wonders. Impressive though these were, his initial attempts at securing the world's attention were met with frustrating, lackluster responses—folk simply did not pay him any mind at first.

Exodus 6:2-7:13 records the prelude to the deliverance. God exhorted a perturbed and deflated eighty-year-old Moses to return to Pharaoh and again petition the monarch to release the Hebrews, with the promise that he would eventually succeed (6:10-17). Exodus 7:14-12:28 notes a host of plagues, ten in all, that culminated in an eventual deliverance from Egypt and subsequent Israelite march to freedom (12:29-51).

In 13:17-15:21, however, readers are informed that the Egyptian monarch had a change of heart and attempted to retrieve his abused wayward slaves, then heading *en masse* toward the border. His plan, however, was thwarted: we're told in 14:15-31 that the Red Sea parted for the escaping Israelites, but then collapsed upon the Egyptian army as they pursued the fleeing Hebrews.

After giving voice to the salvation experience through jubilant song, in 15:1-21, the newly freed people of Israel set their sights south by southwest, and headed to Sinai in 15:22-16:36, where they would later receive their "constitution," their "penal code," their "code of criminal procedures," and their "marching orders" for personal success in life—beginning, of course, with the "Ten Commandments."

Both the Hebrews and Egyptians were amazed by the "Ten Plagues," though the Hebrews fared better than the Egyptians. The "Red Sea" experience, likewise, caused them to marvel, as did signs associated with the giving of the "Ten Commandments." Still, when the excitement over the miraculous events subsided— and enthusiasm always subsides—*the Israelites, sadly, were overcome by the darker side of their undisciplined natures when confronted with the stark realities of their new and perplexing situation.*

Much as Adam and Eve were defeated by their appetites, the Israelites' complaints over hunger in chapter 16 consumed them. They had worried about water purity at Marah in 15:22-27, and faced another water shortage in 17:1-7. Over and again, biblical readers hear the Israelites complaining. Though somewhat similar to Adam and Eve's discontent, there were some major differences: the first couple was in a garden paradise, surrounded by abundance; the three-million-strong Israelites were in a barren wilderness, and they were clueless as to how they would get their next meal.

While moderns tend to be overly critical of the Hebrews for their "whining," we should remember that these three million individuals had just found themselves thrust into a rather inhospitable wilderness and they were experiencing the rapid depletion of much needed, life-sustaining provisions. The logistics associated with attending to their basic food and water needs would dwarf anyone's sensibilities and stretch the material resources of a well-trained modern army attempting to make headway in that, or any, region with sparse natural resources. Beyond all of this, and more importantly, readers must remember that Moses' constituents were recently-freed slaves. Strange as it may sound to independently-minded Americans—whose values prize individuality and autonomy and call forth a host of problem-solving skills—the Israelites were unused to making individual decisions. Neither they nor their immediate ancestors had any life experience in making decisions, acting responsibly, or acquiring resources: remember, for centuries they'd been nothing but oppressed "slave stock."

For many generations, Hebrew slaves in Egypt were dehumanized into thinking and behaving as human beasts of burden. In their own estimation, they were but human work animals, no more. As slaves, their food needs were sufficiently provided for by their overlords, much as the Egyptians' oxen and donkeys were well watered and fed, in order that their masters could derive more utility from their healthy livestock. Slave stock was maintained in Egypt, as well. But what now? What would happen in the wilderness—in their new and

Exodus

inhospitable context, where resources were in high demand, but very short supply? Not only were food staples diminished, but their inclinations were diminished, as well, through centuries of operating with diminished capacities.

Though excited by their recent amazing, providential turn of events, they were uncertain, still. They didn't see the future and weren't even trained to look for it; they had no known scripts to fall back on, either. Though freed from Egypt, they were nevertheless still trapped in something of a phantasmal, ghost-like state: they were driven by excitement about the present on the one hand, and by dread terror of the uncertain future on the other. Though extricated from Egypt, they were stuck in their own dysfunctional, downward-spiraling thought processes.

God's temporarily providing miraculous food staples in the wilderness, in and of itself, did not obviate the logistical problems these newly freed men and women faced. To be sure, God proved to be more than gracious with them—as with us; for, not only did they get a "helping hand" from Heaven with their legitimate food needs, they also experienced miracle-help from Heaven when Moses raised his hands and enabled their inexperienced army to miraculously destroy the Amalekite forces bent on their demise in 17:8-16, shortly after the exodus.

It takes time to reorient thinking. After years of abuse and misery, these ex-slaves weren't used to anyone or anything acting on their behalf. Here now, however, an unfamiliar God adopted them and became their champion. These were extremely strange days for the Hebrews—to put it mildly. They did not "catch on" right away.

47

Guns & Moses

God was their savior and provider, true; but His tending to their needs didn't re-wire their negative thought processes. They were, in many respects, "thrown to the wolves," and it took them some time to come to terms with their new world. As one might well imagine, they didn't do well at the first.

Transitions—deaths, separations, divorces, unemployment, refugee status, and the like—are times of uncertainty, and throw the people involved into precarious and frustrating situations.

Those who come upon such people—and there are many such people in our unstable world—do well to be as gracious internally, and kindly disposed interpersonally, as their dispositions and vocations permit. God certainly was patient, given the foibles of the recalcitrant people He was working with. *Though Scripture rebukes them for their non-compliance and faithlessness, God maintains patience and faithfulness toward them.*

Remembering the Israelites' circumstances, we can cut them some slack: They had experienced years of dire poverty, had entered a season of extreme uncertainty, and suffered serious logistical problems. Furthermore, they were following a relatively unknown God (Jehovah), a relatively new and untested leader (Moses), and were headed to an entirely unknown place (Canaan). Those who work with disconcerted people often experience these people at their absolute worst, as difficult and flustered individuals who easily become emotionally frayed, reactive, and unreasonable. They are often at or near their "wits end" emotionally and intellectually, and can be just plain angry—sometimes even at those trying to help them. Better that the helpers remain kindly disposed and not too reactive. It takes time to change, and we do well to allow folk to move at their own pace—not ours.

Exodus

The Israelites' bad behavior was attributed, in part, simply to their not knowing any better: a different way of being had never been modeled for them. They needed proactive assistance and not reactive resistance—and the needed help was on its way.

Speaking of help, in chapter 18, Moses' non-Jewish, Bedouin father-in-law, Jethro, visited Moses and encouraged him to appoint some elders to assist him with vexing and time-consuming administrative tasks. That Moses heeded his non-Hebrew, Bedouin father-in-law reminds us that we all have blind spots in our thinking and can derive benefit from wisdom resident in folk outside the clan. We should be open to others! Moses' being so didn't compromise his biblical virtue in the least.

The Ten Commandments
Moving along, readers learn that three months into the journey, the children of Israel finally reached Mount Sinai (19:1), where Moses ascended the mountain's heights (vv. 2-25) to get a hold of God's wisdom to help re-wire God's once-vanquished people. There, Moses initially received an abbreviated version of God's "Law," God's manifest will for a just and orderly human society.

At this point in the Exodus narrative, readers are spared one pathetic piece of information: when Moses ascended the mountain, those remaining at the base abandoned Moses and Jehovah outright, and proceeded to manufacture a "Golden Calf," which then became the object of their misguided religious affections. Moses postpones this account until chapter 32, where he follows it in chapters 33 and 34 with the story of his mediation and the manufacture of a second set of tablets. We first come upon the Commandments' particulars in chapter 20.

Guns & Moses

Commandments one through four of the set of ten affirm God's personhood, forbid both the manufacture of idols and the defamation of God's Holy Name, and set aside a special Sabbath day, a day of worship and rest (20:1-8). The requirement to observe a "day off" is embellished in verses 9-11, which inform that the Sabbath rest even applied to cattle, as well as to human employees: in the new economy everyone and everything deserved "a break." The concerns of commandments six through ten are social in nature, as distinct from one through four, which are spiritual, denoting Hebrews' principal obligations toward God.

Following religious duties toward God (e.g., don't take His Name in vain, honor the Sabbath, etc.), number five explicitly requires that individuals respect their parents (v. 12). Commandments six through ten forbid brazenly taking human life ("Thou shalt not murder"), wantonly disregarding others' personal boundaries through illicit sexual contact ("adultery"), maliciously acquiring another's goods ("stealing/theft"), committing perjury ("bearing false witness"), and coveting another's relationships or property (vv. 13-17). This last inclination triggered the events in the Garden of Eden and many ills thereafter.

That individuals' boundaries and property rights were to be respected would be good news, indeed, to individuals accustomed to degrading servitude, where they were disrespected property themselves, and little more.

We can only imagine that the Israelites, having suffered grievously for hundreds of years under the unpredictable whims of oppressive overlords, would especially appreciate God's premium on human dignity.

Exodus

Owing to the premium placed on the *dignity of every man* and the harmful social and spiritual effect of intimidating servitude, *ongoing institutional slavery was prohibited for Israelites in the new economy* (21:2-11). One could hire oneself out as "short term" field or domestic labor, only; but Hebrews were not to accept perpetual servile status. In the Mosaic economy female servants were kindly granted civil rights and protections unavailable to such women elsewhere (vv. 7-11). *Paramount in the new social constitution was the inherent dignity of every person, the weak and the strong alike—an inalienable right that was to be held inviolate, irrespective of one's race or class,* something that applied to Jew and non-Jew alike.

More prohibitions against "murder" follow in verses 12-14, and are worthy of amplification, given that the mandate is often misunderstood. Translating the sixth commandment as "Thou shalt not *kill*" does *not* communicate the intention of the writer, as it is not born out in the original language. A more accurate translation would read, "Thou shalt not *murder.*"

Given the nature of the world that Moses inhabited (and our world also), there come times when it is necessary for individuals to legitimately bear arms in defense of home and hearth; for to cower in fear would be to abrogate one's fundamental responsibility as a citizen, not to mention one's own duty as a human being.

To "take up for oneself "and "fight" is not a privilege granted to slaves—who must suffer in silence, with no recourse and absolutely no hope of securing redress for grievances. Brazen disregard for life through "murder" is, of course, unacceptable; however, protecting life and property—even to the point of killing—is not eschewed, myths to the contrary aside. Being able to fight is a right—and a good one at that.

"Use of force"—and "deadly force," particularly—for legitimate ends is not only tolerated in biblical literature, it is actually celebrated in the Old Testament. In the Texts, warriors become heroes, such as King David, Gideon, and many, many others. At issue in the Commandments is the employment of deadly force, driven by the passion and anger of self-serving persons who pay no mind to justice, but use force for their own ends. This wanton disregard for basic rights is eschewed outright, as men are required to govern their persons and not to be overrun by their internal base and selfish tendencies. Still, bearing arms legitimately is not condemned.

Speaking of self-government, individuals are again reminded by Moses to govern their dispositions and respect their parents (vv. 15, 17), as they were previously exhorted to do in the fifth of the "Ten Commandments."

Should one be unable or unwilling to marshal the internal resources necessary to show respect toward one's own parents, how would one marshal the energies necessary to respect other legitimate authorities, such as teachers, employers, and law enforcement officials? Simply put, the inability to respect one's parents—and one hopes that the parents act respectably themselves—destines one to a non-life, functioning only as a participant in society's leeching underclasses where diseased and disoriented individuals prey on others and use them as utilities to satisfy their wandering desires. This is not what God would have for His people, who must live under a mandate to respect human life in all its forms—beginning in the home. Respecting all life forms prompts individuals to respect all persons, irrespective of their race, class, religion, etc.

Exodus

Verses 18-27 deal with intentional assaults, injuries to pregnant women, and injuries to servants; verses 28-32 deal with accidental injuries. Chapter 21:33-22:14 takes up injuries through neglect (vv. 33-34), through theft (21:37-22:3), and through accidental damages caused by cattle and fire (vv. 4-14). These verses, along with those following, amplify the "Ten Commandments."

Sexual improprieties are dealt with in 22:16-17, followed by the eradication of witchcraft (vv. 18, 20). Sexual relations with animals are expressly prohibited in verse 19, as is oppressing weaker humans in verses 21-24. Loans to the poor were to be governed with grace and handled in a way that did not present undue hardship to the one to whom the loan was extended (vv. 25-27): *here again, the importance of assisting the marginalized and dispossessed is stressed.* Perjury is prohibited in 23:1-3, as is consorting with deceitful and wicked fellows, generally.

In like manner, Israelites were told to not "lower themselves" and not behave like their enemies in the process of dealing with them (vv. 4-5). While speaking of dealing with others prudently, Moses goes on to say that those vested with juridical authority must be impartial in the employment of their judgment (vv. 6-9), and not moved by attractive bribes (v. 8). Sacred holidays were to be observed (vv. 10-18), spending was to be mitigated with tithing, and dietary laws were to be maintained (v. 19). All said, in 24:12 God reminds Moses that this is the law that he is to deliver and teach.

Specific mandates germane to the Tabernacle's construction were given in 25:1-27:19, 29:38-30:10, 30:11-31:18, 35:4-38:20; particulars of the construction were given in 38:21-31. One observes instructions for Tabernacle service and servants in 27:20-28:43, the priesthood's consecration in 29:1-37, and even their garments' manufacture in 39:1-22. The construction was completed in 39:33-43, after which Moses describes the Tabernacle's ordination and consecration in chapter 40.

Summary and Lessons Learned

To be "civilized" denotes having one's base appetites and tendencies controlled. One must, by definition, act "civil" in order to secure a place in a "civilization." Self-government enables unrelated and diverse people to live close by each other, and helps fellow citizens interact with mutual respect while servicing common interests and needs. *Self-government is the hallmark of civilization,* much as its absence gives rise to barbaric actions and society's decline.

An explicit and agreed-upon social contract goes hand in hand with a civilized society. This contract articulates common expectations and delineates the benefits of compliance, as well as the punishments associated with non-compliance.

What make the Mosaic Law unique are *not* the mandates to "not kill," "not steal," avoid "adultery," or honor a lord; for these mandates can be found in other religions far-removed from biblical literature and influence. *Unique, rather, is the religious premium that the "Law" places on assisting distressed and dispossessed persons,* and the *equity* that is mandated for *all* people across the board—for the rich and poor alike.

In Moses' Law, people are considered *"righteous"* when they treat other people *"rightly,"* much as their being deemed "unrighteous" is indicative of their dealing "unrightly" with others. This dealing unrightly is often observed with Muslim zealots today who, in their religion's name, take life and property with brazen disregard for basic human rights: they show no regard for the non-combatant aged, for children, or for women. Such practices need condemnation by all religions—period!

Laws are typically manufactured by those in a society's powerful classes, and are often written to self-service the needs and interests of those in the classes who wield the social power. By way of contrast and distinction, *the Mosaic economy does not favor the powerful, but is inclined toward the disenfranchised*—to be sure, an interesting and innovative development in ancient religion. Over and again, readers are told to be kindly disposed toward the "stranger," the "alien," and the "poor"—today's unfortunate refugees; and folk back then were reminded that they themselves were once slaves in the land of Egypt. I wish that these principles governed the affairs of all today!

Thus is introduced an unprecedented shift in social ethics—itself the genius of the Divinely-inspired Mosaic revelation. In Psalm 15, David reflected on the virtue that resonates from the unbiased "Law." I quote it here as a fitting conclusion to this chapter and as a passageway to Leviticus:

"Lord, who may abide in Your tabernacle? Who may dwell in Your holy hill? He who *walks uprightly*, and *works righteousness*, and *speaks the truth in his heart*; He who *does not backbite with his tongue, nor does evil to his neighbor, nor does take up a reproach against his friend*; In whose eyes *a vile person is despised*. But he *honors those who fear the Lord*; He who *swears to his own hurt and does not change*; He who *does not put out his money at usury, nor does he take a bribe against the innocent. He who does these things shall never be moved.*"

III

Leviticus

Introduction

First known by the title "Law of the Priests," Leviticus considers the manifold functions of the newly constituted priesthood, which came into being with the Tabernacle's construction. The word "priest" usually conjures an image of a spiritual leader officiating in and serving the "church"—as distinct from the "state." This picture obscures the civil nature and purposes of the biblically sanctioned vocation in antiquity. The new worship site created the need for religiously trained individuals to attend to it, and the priesthood carried religious and sacerdotal responsibilities. But, to manage the swelling population's particular needs and interests, a class of jurists, medical professionals, and inspectors had to emerge. The multimillion member community's juridical needs were felt immediately; therefore, by way of response, the educated priests were vested with responsibility to serve as the community's jurists—lawyers, judges, and the like—and not just as spiritual advisors, as today.

In the interest of helping establish good, godly government, Leviticus deals with these and other domains related to the soul. Contrary to popular myth, Mosaic religion didn't allow guilt-ridden Israelites to settle accounts with their consciences by simply offering up animal sacrifices in religious rites at religious sites. The Israelites first had to do personal or social penance and make restitution for the wrong(s) committed. Leviticus underscores this.

A holy and religious life as laid out in Leviticus was a moral life as it instructed Israelites to attend to their ethical obligations and "rights" in conjunction with the various ceremonial "rites."

At the head of it all, the Levite tribe served as the moral and legal guides of the community.

Exposition of Leviticus

Leviticus first notes various Tabernacle offerings, all of which Moses explains in the book's opening chapters, one through seven. Burnt offerings (chapter 1), Grain offerings (chapter 2), Peace offerings (chapter 3), Sin offerings (chapter 4), and Trespass offerings (chapters 5-7) precede specified duties for the priests to perform regarding the respective sacrificial gifts.

Chapter 8 takes up the formal consecration of Aaron and his sons to the priesthood. They were to be washed, clothed, and anointed. Sacrifices were to be offered on their behalf, the blood of which was to be symbolically placed on each priest's ear, thumb, and toe: the ear, to accentuate his need to *hear* God's Word; the thumb to denote the premium on *doing*

Leviticus

God's Work, and the toe to indicate a willingness to *go* where God leads—emphasis on real-world activity, not mere contemplation (though contemplation is important). Then, in 9:1-22, after consecration, the priests entered their offices with sacrifices, followed by God's fiery response in verses 23-24.

No One Above the Law

Such ritual conferred upon the leadership a sacred trust, and those who were elevated to the sacred vocation of executing the Law's particulars received added respect, "pomp," and behavior standards.

The priesthood's serious nature was evidenced by the summary execution of the High Priest's own wanton sons, Nadab and Abihu, in 10:1-7. Thinking that their father's position entitled them to special liberties proved fatal for the two boys—as with ministers' kids who assume they have similar entitlement today—for both sons were consumed by fire in the Tabernacle after igniting God's disapproval with their brazen disregard for worship decorum. Their untimely deaths reminded all that the priesthood was serious business, not to be approached casually—no exceptions. Everyone must play by the same rules!

In like manner, *their deaths supported and promoted the contention that there were to be no privileged people or classes in Israel.*

There were no special exemptions and special privileges: everyone had to follow the Mosaic standards—including those born into the culture's higher social strata, who might assume they had special entitlements and exemptions. No one was above the Law—neither then, nor now. Leviticus dictates *common standards of law for all citizens, irrespective of social standing. This is an important hallmark of Mosaic Law.*

Drunkenness

The prohibition against drinking in the Tabernacle that follows in verses 8-11 suggests that Aaron's upper class sons may have been inebriated when committing their offense.

Drunkenness itself was a problem in antiquity—same as today. The severe punishment, in this case, is an indicator that its dangers were perceived at the dawn of our religious civilization, as during Noah's day. Genesis readers may recall that Noah became inebriated, with ill effects.

Diet

Miscellaneous dietary restrictions follow the prohibition against drunkenness, in chapter 11, detailing consumption of acceptable land mammals (vv. 1-8), fish (vv. 9-12), birds (vv. 13-19) and winged, swarming creatures (vv. 20-23). Given the importance of caring for our bodies, Moses considers health issues such as defilement through contacting the dead, in verses 24-28, and unclean creeping things, in verses 29-43. Chapters 12-15 pertain to childbirth (12), leprosy (13-14) and bodily secretions (15)—all health-code related, and very real-world.

In chapter 16, Moses mentions the deaths of his nephews, Nadab and Abihu, before describing the regulations for the most sacred of Tabernacle worship, "Day of Atonement."

After a reminder that worship is serious and not to be taken lightly, the particulars for the day's activities begin. Sacerdotal activities came with sacrificial animals and instructions for the management of sacrifices (vv. 3-34). At the height of this special day, the High Priest would enter into the Holy of Holies with

Leviticus

blood in hand and make atonement for Israel's sins—thus the "Day of Atonement." New Testament readers recognize a strong connection between this activity and the ministry of Jesus, Himself the "High Priest of our Confession," according to more than one New Testament writer.

Sexual Improprieties
Picking up on health-related concerns again, along with mandates to be separate and distinct from neighboring populations, chapter 17 follows by considering the slaying of animals for food, reminding that blood was not to be consumed by humans (vv. 10-14). Then, in the wake of exhortations toward holiness, forbidden marriages are noted and eschewed outright in 18:6-8, as are sexual improprieties generally, in verses 9-19. Moses did not appreciate sexual experimentation and states emphatically that homosexuality is not acceptable for God's covenant people. "Thou shalt not lie with a man as with a woman," he says in verse 22. Later, 20:13 prescribes a penalty for such activity.

So as not to single out homosexual liaisons, Moses also condemns incestuous relationships (vv. 6-18), along with other expressions of sexual impropriety, illicit heterosexual ones particularly. Moses warns that sexual improprieties can be addictive and tend toward the defilement of individuals and communities. "Keep My statutes and ordinances and you shall *not* do any of these…" he says on God's behalf (vv. 26-28). Would that these were heeded today!

Individuals are *not* given free reign to experiment with any and all manner of sexual experience, *à la* "What consensual adults do in their bedrooms is their own business." Heterosexual fornication is not accepted. Those who argue for the acceptance of homosexuality do not draw their support from either the synagogue's or church's traditional literature, which sanction marriage—one man, one woman. The biblical economy legitimizes monogamous relationships between the Adams and Eves of the world, not the Adams and Steves!

Summary of the Torah

Chapter 19 occupies the central portion of Leviticus and is *the linguistic center* of the entire Mosaic economy. Judaism's rabbis have long noted, "The essentials of the Torah are noted therein." Thus, this chapter is traditionally perceived as a counterpart to the "Decalogue"—i.e., the "Ten Commandments" (Exodus 20). The Pentateuch's Author (God) obviously considers Israel's constitution of such importance that He revisits the principal commandments here.

As with Exodus' "Ten Commandments," the fundamental moral laws to honor parents, keep Sabbaths, and eschew idols are noted in 19:3-4, followed by a reminder to comply with some of the essential ritual laws in verses 5-8. The imperative to "remember the poor" is noted in verses 9-10, as are *obligations toward fellow men* generally in 11-16. Don't "steal" (v. 11), don't swear falsely" (v. 12), don't "cheat" or "rob" (v. 13), and don't hinder the handicapped (v. 14) remind readers of the premium that business-related virtue plays for those embraced by biblical religion. In fact, prudent dealings with all people, in all situations, are encouraged: *"You shall do no injustice in judgment. You shall not be partial to the poor, nor honor the person of the mighty. In righteousness you shall judge your neighbor"* (v. 15).

This same principle is applied later in the chapter to "aliens"— who, being social "outsiders," would find themselves ill protected.

Further prohibitions include spreading gossip and slander (v. 16), bearing grudges (v. 17), and taking vengeance (v. 18). The

Leviticus

commandment that follows—prohibiting the mixing of linen fabrics and animal skins—likely reminded the Israelites that they were not to assimilate, and thus get too mixed up with those in the surrounding cultures. They were to remain separate and distinct (v. 19). Later, in verse 27, God required males to cut their hair in a distinguishable fashion, possibly to keep His men's appearance different, so as not to be unduly attractive to foreign women. In any event, a prohibition against sexual indiscretion in verses 20-22 offers the appropriate remedies of scourging and sacrifice. Interestingly, Moses then jumps to a crop management policy in verses 23-26 (and 25:1-11), after which he again reiterates the imperative not to eat food containing blood (v. 26). Tattoos are eschewed in verse 28, likely because of their association with the pagan cults then, and the mandate to keep daughters from prostitution is stressed in verse 29.

Sexual improprieties and false religion go hand in hand in biblical literature—both here and elsewhere. (See "Disobedience = Consequences" on p. 87 of this book.) Verse 31 commands, "Give no regard to mediums," and "do not seek after them." Lastly, the reminder to "rise before the gray-headed and honor the presence of the old man" in verse 32 reminds of the imperative to honor the elderly, a disposition not universally appreciated in America's youth-oriented, sin-soaked culture. Other cultures show greater appreciation. I understand that Arabs, for example, do a better job with this imperative.

Moses closes the summary of the Torah by harking back to the obligation to be forthright in dealing with others, e.g., to not "steal," perjure, commit theft or robbery, or molest the weak. *The ethical mandates that bind Hebrews to deal honorably with each other, extend that business ethic to their dealings with non-Israelites*—an ethical innovation and evidence of the Torah's genius.

Treat Others as Brothers

As mentioned previously, strangers among the Israelites would find themselves in ill-protected positions, given their not having tight associations in the area where they reside: "the stranger who dwells among you shall be to you as one born among you, and you shall love him as yourself; for you were strangers in the land of Egypt: *I am the Lord* your God" (v. 34). This and other mandates prohibit Israelis from hating and mistreating Arabic peoples—living among or in proximity to Jews—and tacitly compel Jewish people to respect those who worship according to the dictates of their own consciences. This includes those who wish to practice any religion or no religion at all. Respect is of paramount importance, affording people the privilege to live their own lives unmolested by the powers that be.

The premium on justice—and "justice for *all!*"—leaps out at us. Verses 35-37 further articulate this hallmark of Mosaic Law: "You shall do no injustice in judgment, in measurement of length, weight or volume. You shall have honest scales, honest weights... *I am the Lord* your God, who brought you out of the land of Egypt. Therefore you shall observe all My statutes and all My judgments, and perform them: *I am the Lord.*" Again, being honest, non-manipulative, and respecting others are religious obligations, not just social ones. Good business becomes a religious obligation.

More will be said about the nature of evenhanded "justice" later. The oft-repeated expression, "I am the Lord," is worth exploring here: it is arguably repeated to underscore the fact that God Himself is the ultimate judge of all matters—and thus takes note whether justice is administrated successfully, in accordance with His revealed will.

He is the Lord—the ultimate authority and magistrate. He truly is, and if Moses' words are given any weight it becomes clear that all people must give an accounting to that Magistrate, in part, on the basis of how they lived out the ethical mandates articulated in His laws. That said, *men and women would all do well to cultivate justice and virtue in dealings with other people, and eschew vice and avarice outright,* seeing these as enemies to our souls. Leviticus presents *sin as both a personal and communal nemesis, and not just a personal religious problem*—as it is typically "marketed" in Evangelical, American culture.

Higher Standards for Those in Authority
Chapter 21 addresses the conduct of priests, whose standards must be "above reproach."

Ministering Levites, "in service," worked as judges—and not just as spiritual and family counselors. As such, they dealt with a variety of people and a full range of civil and criminal matters, in addition to their being the guardians and gatekeepers of the religious tradition and condition of Israel, as with rabbis (24:10-23 and 27:1-33).

There was no distinction between "church" and "state" then. What we would label "religious" mandates had the effect of a binding social constitution, which guided the judges to discern the essential "elements of offenses" in civil and criminal matters, much as our Penal Code does. It also denoted our Code of Criminal Procedure, giving those vested with authority their rules of enforcement.

Because the Levitical priests served as jurists, they needed to be held to higher standards. While this was true for the priests, generally, it was particularly true for the "Chief Priest" or "High Priest." He was to be an unblemished person, one who conducted himself honorably in his public appearances, and who kept his private life unsullied (21:10-15; ch. 22) so as to be a role model for others. Along with their various juridical functions, priests were assigned sacerdotal duties in conjunction with Israel's sacred schedule of feasts and seasons (ch. 23; 24:1-9; 25:1-11).

Dignity of the Individual

Just prior to giving his closing admonition, Moses reminds readers of the imperative to *remember the poor* (25:25-38) and, in no uncertain terms, *not to dishonor the poor by forcing them into degrading servitude.*

Because all humankind was made in "God's image and likeness," *all human beings are understood to have inherent dignity* and high status, irrespective of their ethnic origin, looks, wealth, or position in life—and *irrespective of whether they be a Muslim, Christian, Jew, or otherwise related*; and all are to be afforded the inalienable rights which come with their elevated standing—being a superior creation, bearing God's very own seal, personal approval, and "likeness." Even in weakness, humans are still considered to be "a little lower than angels" (Ps. 8). "Fallen" though we indeed may be, those who deal with sin-weakened humankind, and who decide upon social matters between men and women, do well to remember this lofty principle; for failing to do so will prove disastrous to those who misuse power.

Leviticus

Obey...or Else!

Chapter 26:3-44 promises blessings for obedience to the laws, along with curses for insolence.

Compliance carries with it the promise of Divine aid, which will translate into financial success for faithful adherents (vv. 4-5). The faithful are promised "peace in the land" (v. 6) and that their enemies will "fall by the sword" (vv. 6-8, esp. v. 7). God says that He "will look on you favorably and make you fruitful [and] multiply you" (v. 9), noting: "I will walk among you and be your God, and you shall be My people" (v. 12). God promises to bless and prosper the righteous—good news, for sure.

God, in like manner, also promises to harangue the unrighteous—those who deal unrightly with others—and cause them to regret the day they ventured out of their mothers' wombs. That He is the God of the poor and oppressed—folk humbled by life's circumstances who *must* still be respected!—is noted at the close of His promised blessings: "I am your God, who brought you out of the land of Egypt, that you should not be their slaves; I have broken the bands of your yoke and made you walk upright" (v. 13). Having been "given a break," Israelites should be so inclined toward others.

In sum, *the initial kindness shown by God toward the Israelites must be reflected in the Israelites' dealings with others—*particularly, those weaker and, thus, less fortunate; failure to do so would bring dire consequences. Should the Israelites abuse their newfound freedoms and not be kindly disposed toward those less fortunate in their various social dealings with them, or should they violate other sacred principles, they would surely face the prospects of Divine retribution! This was not the preferred scenario.

Righteousness wasn't privatized; it entailed being rightly disposed toward others—even those outside the tribe.

"[I]f you do *not* obey Me, and do not observe all these commandments," reported Moses (on God's behalf), "and you despise My statutes, or if your soul abhors My [ethical] judgments, so that you do not perform all My commandments...," I will do this to you: "I will appoint terror over you, wasting disease and fever" (v. 16), "I will set My face against you, you shall be defeated by your enemies, [and] those who hate you will reign over you" (v. 17). "I will punish you seven times more for your sins" (v. 18) and will "break the pride of your power" (v. 19), such that "your strength will be spent in vain" (v. 20), and "I will lay your cities waste" (v. 31). Verses 21-39 continue, noting explicitly that compliance with the Mosaic constitution is required, "or else."

Leviticus thus closes with a firm and fitting reminder that the priests were expected to see to it that the ethical injunctions contained in the Torah were applied to the practice of everyday life, and in everyday interactions with people; for failure to do so equitably, says Moses, would bring certain devastation and ultimate ruin to those who abused others.

Summary and Lessons Learned

The correlation between religious faith toward God and ethical/righteous conduct in interacting with *all* humans is astounding in Leviticus, and was unprecedented in recorded human history.

The importance of doing "right" over merely practicing religious "rite" contributes toward Judaism's self-understanding and the nature of Israelite religion.

Leviticus

Whereas many refer to Mosaic religion as "monotheism"—meaning "one God"—some Hebrews employ the adjective "ethical," hence, the preferred designation is "ethical monotheism," highlighting the premium on virtue toward fellow man that is accentuated in the ethics-based Mosaic Code and of paramount importance throughout Old Testament religion—as in the New. We see this emphasis on ethics elsewhere in the Law and prophets, and again in the New Testament.

The Apostle Paul referred to the "Law" as a "school master," literally a "boy leader." This may recollect a tradition of some Jewish sages (teachers) who began the day by taking lads to school—denoting the emphasis that Jews place on education. Jewish youngsters "cut their teeth" intellectually on Leviticus, this book being the primer employed to teach reading to children. Leviticus deserves to be more than a schoolbook for the Jewish young; Leviticus is a summary and reiteration of essential biblical truths that form ethical conduct. We adults do well to read it, paying special attention to the ethical imperatives that bear directly on the use of power.

IV

Numbers

Introduction

Whereas Leviticus is largely legislative in nature—dealing with civil and criminal regulations and with sacerdotal functions related to the Sanctuary—the Book of Numbers spends more energy on historical narrative, as did Genesis and Exodus. As a result, it reads less like a law "code" and more like a swift-moving story—and what a meaningful story it is.

Genesis follows Abraham's promise through his progeny, a small clan, moving about between Mesopotamia and Egypt. Come Exodus, the small group had evolved into a formidable nation-state, and miraculously secured a victory over harsh Egyptian overlords.

Guns & Moses

The freed, ragtag slaves fled Egypt and were led by Moses to Sinai, where they received a basic "Constitution"—a social contract to serve as the hallmark for their fresh, new civilization. Armed with an understanding of what was expected of them by their sovereign Lord (and each other), they were ready to leave Mount Sinai and set their sights northward, toward Canaan, to claim their destiny with promises of God acting as their strong patron. Based on a literal reading of the Pentateuch, reasonable estimates put the Exodus population as high as over three million, with a fighting force of over 600,000.

Numbers tells the story of their journey—recounting their miseries along the way. It is called *"BaMidbar"* in Hebrew, meaning, "[wandering] in the wilderness." The wilderness journey, as we shall see, was tragically checkered by disintegration, despair, decay, and various other sorts of social and spiritual degradation. For the first generation of freed Israelites, it's a horrible story—a story of life gone bad. But, it's a story with implications for us in the modern world.

Chapter 1:1-10:11 tells of the first census, the selection of Levites, means of dealing with jealous husbands (to curb domestic assaults), and more. Chapter 10:12-chapter 21 tells of myriad challenges to Moses, personally. Moses' character and authority were challenged by family (chapter 12) and friends (chapter 16). Gripping fear of the Canaanites, Moses tells us, condemned the Israelites to an abysmal life of seemingly aimless wandering, until the initial generation died off and paved the way for their children to initiate, attain, and maintain the long-anticipated conquest. Chapters 22-36 describe the journey's "tail end" and will be the object of some attention later on.

Exposition of Numbers

The Text begins in 1:1-4:20 with the taking of a census to ascertain Israel's fighting strength, followed by a non-military numerical assessment in 4:21-49. Tally the troops though they may, God meant to be understood as their source of pride and success—a lesson all too commonly forgotten by those determined to rely on their own prowess.

Because success would be attributed to Divine favor and not just by the dint of their own dogged determination, Israel was given instructions on dealing with defiled persons in 5:1-4, followed by instructions for the need for repentant persons to make restitution toward parties injured by them (vv. 5-10). People were not to live in sin and expect that God would continue to support their endeavors. Would that we all lived with the fear of God's displeasure!

The rules for a "Trial by Ordeal" follow in verses 11-31, a custom that many moderns find unacceptable and use to argue that the Sacred Text discriminates against women.

Angry and jealous husbands, vexed by concerns that their wives were having secret, sexual liaisons with other men, were given parameters within which they had to operate to learn the truth. The jealous man was to bring his accused wife to the priest (vv. 11-15), who would prepare a beverage for the suspected spouse to drink (v. 16). The priest would pray a particular curse upon her should she have been unfaithful (vv. 17-22), and then require her to drink the mixture. If she had "behaved unfaithfully," Moses says the drink would become "bitter, and her belly will swell, and her thigh will rot, and the woman will become a curse among her people" (v. 27)—i.e., she would manifest symptoms construed as evidence of her unfaithfulness, and suffer accordingly. If innocent of the charge—if she showed none of the signs—she would be free.

This practice, called a "Trial by Ordeal," is understandably unacceptable to moderns. I grant that it seems problematic until we examine it further.

Barbaric as this may seem at first glance, note the hedge that it provided against unmitigated rage and jealousy in households; for, if a man felt that he was being wronged and cheated upon, he was required to *prove his case publicly*, and not just rage against a victimized spouse in the privacy of his home. The mandate, no doubt, prompted many men to bridle their accusations, for the wife could always insist she be taken to the priest where the man would be made a fool of publicly when she was exonerated by the "Ordeal." As a result, *what might seem like a process that denigrated women actually served to promote their security* and well-being, protecting them from a husband's unfounded suspicions and unbridled anger. Here, as elsewhere, *protecting the less powerful is showcased as the hallmark of biblical religion.*

Sabbatical Retreats
Because life can—and oftentimes does—become complicated for married men and women alike, individuals need to vacate, to "get away," sometimes and regroup. The "Law of the Nazarite," noted in 6:1-21, gives specific instructions for these occasional retreats: participants were not to drink wine (vv. 3-4), they were not to cut their hair (v. 5), and were not to go to funerals (v. 6-12). The point being that they were on a "religious retreat" for a season and, thus, were to be temporarily removed from their ever-pressing, worldly concerns.

Numbers

The wise have long noted the importance of "getting away." The word "recreation" comes from the term "re-create," meaning to "create anew." Individuals' inner constitutions are, in many respects, created afresh when they temporarily vacate their everyday, challenging, workaday worlds. Much as a computer can "freeze" or "get jammed" and prompt the owner to "shut it down" and "re-boot it," so, too, humans need to turn off the engines of their lives and restart them—take a sabbatical rest.

It is good to "step back" sometimes from the day's pressing problems, regroup, and gain new perspective, is it not? (Hopefully, this book enables readers to do just that: gain new perspectives—biblical ones—germane to dealing with vexing, earthly concerns.)

A troubled Moses, as one might recall, was himself forced to "get away" from Egypt for a season. Eventually, he experienced the "call" by a "burning bush" and returned. Invigorated as he was, and instructed as well, he proceeded to apply his energies in the new direction and the rest is biblical history.

The need to "step back," "get away," and "recharge" is very important, and was institutionalized and sanctioned in the concept of the "Nazarite Vow."

As we shall see later in this chapter, working with people can be extremely disorienting, and the need to recover equilibrium is stressed, especially for professions relating to people or authority. Instructions follow in chapter 7 for leaders' offerings, the Tabernacle's sacred light—the "menorah"—and the Levites' dedication (chapter 8), and the Passover celebration for defiled persons (9:1-14). The section closes with an indication of God's presence in the Tabernacle, a sure sign of His favor (vv. 15-23).

With this accomplished, the Israelites were ready to journey from the sacred mountain to the Holy Land, to Israel—the mysterious land vouchsafed forever as their land of biblical promise. Chapter 10:11-36 offers an account of the orderly journey from Mount Sinai to the land of Israel.

Transitions Cause Stress

The group may have looked splendid as they marched ever onward and upward toward the Holy Land, but all was not well. Rank disorder soon became apparent and tragically marked the day along the way.

The people complained and craved in 11:1-35. "Who will give us meat to eat?" they lamented (v. 4). "We remember the fish we ate freely in Egypt, the cucumbers, the melons, the leeks, the onions... and now our being is dried up; there is nothing except this manna before our eyes," they exclaimed (vv. 5-6). *They complained, and the "Lawgiver" Moses, time and again, got the brunt of it.*

Fish, cucumbers, leeks, and melons in abundance! Sounds great, does it not? From their lamentations, the Israelites make their experience in Egypt sound splendid, as if they were staying at a resort or on an extended cruise where the good food just kept on coming. A review of Exodus, however, confirms that they were *enslaved* in Egypt (not vacationing!), and laboring under an insensitive taskmaster who required much of them and gave little in return.

As we discussed in Exodus 17, *perspectives often become skewed when individuals suffer the pressures created by transitions.* The Israelites' frustration caused by their changed circumstances prompted them to become disoriented—to *misread reality*—

and to rewrite their own history in the process, a problem for people today as much as for people yesterday.

The lesson for those who deal with people in frustrating, uncertain circumstances is to understand this tendency and not to personalize it when those soul-sickened people lash out and speak unfairly. This predictable reaction to unwanted change occurs whether the problems are of their own making or another's. It's human nature, like the tendency to fret, generally. By way of application, *displaced persons—refugees, for example—will not be known for their keen and balanced perspectives, given pressure associated with their abysmal circumstances.* Those who interact with them would do well to appreciate this, in advance, and develop the aptitude to act accordingly.

Racism and Discrimination Condemned

Moses' problems with these disconcerted folk paled in comparison to the problem that came next. The saying that "there is no fight quite like a family fight" serves as a fitting introduction to the next section—where Moses' racist sister Miriam and his all-too-pliable brother Aaron "took him on" personally.

The Text says, "Then Miriam and Aaron spoke against Moses because of the Ethiopian woman whom he had married; for he had married an Ethiopian woman" (12:1). At issue, says Moses, was their irritation—voiced primarily by Miriam—over his having brought a dark-skinned, Ethiopian wife into the family. The Lord's response in verses 9-13 is entertaining: Miriam "became leprous, as white as snow" (v. 10). Upon seeing this and recognizing God's judgment of their remarks and disdain for Moses because of his affections for this "colored" woman, Aaron pleaded with Moses: "Oh, my lord! Please do not lay this sin upon us..." (vv. 11-12). And Moses prayed for them. Miriam was healed in verse 13, but received a mild punishment in verses 14-16.

This example is published, in part, to remind Hebrews—and all Godly people—that we are not to tolerate race-based prejudice, or any other sort for that matter. Evenhanded justice for *all* is the mandate, irrespective of race, class, or whatever.

Moses' "big sister" had accompanied him as an infant, walking alongside the banks of the river as her baby brother floated down the Nile in a hastily manufactured basket-boat. This same Miriam's song is remembered in biblical literature as she jubilantly gave voice to God's triumph at the Red Sea! But what have we here? Moses notes she was a bit *racist*? Miriam? The answer is "Yes."

That Miriam and the High Priest Aaron succumbed to discrimination underscores the fact that *prejudice exists in the human condition.* If we deny that fact, we can't ferret out the prejudice and eradicate it.

It could be true of this book's readers as well. Don't deny it; get rid of it! We are not allowed to hate the black, the white, the brown, the yellow, the Arab, the Muslim, the Jew, the Christian, or those of different persuasions—period!

Isaac's wife Rebekah, in the Genesis narrative, went on record complaining that her dear son Jacob better not marry the unfit women in the area: "If Jacob takes a wife of the daughters of Heth, like these who are the daughters of the land, what good will my life be to me?," she complained (Gen. 27:46). She is on record "throwing a fit," saying, in effect, "I simply can't stand the women around here. If my son Jacob marries one of these Bedouin girls I'm going to kill myself—if not him!" She was not alone, for even Isaac was not fond of those other women—the Hittite girls (Gen. 26:34, 35).

When one remembers the biblical mandate to treat kindly *all* others—including *non*-Israelite "aliens"—the issue surfacing here is less surprising. The Sacred Text addresses it so that the Author can help His readers appreciate that *there is no room for this manner of thinking in biblical virtue.*

That dictum applies even today: Jews are not allowed to discriminate against or hate anyone—including Muslims—categorically, despite the fact that Islam makes much of hating Jews. Though Jews are referred to in Islamic religious literature as "apes" and "pigs" and "slaves," better that Bible readers not categorize Muslims as such: it's just not the Jewish (or Christian) way—period.

Lack of Confidence Dooms Israelites to Wander
With this point made abundantly clear, Moses picks up the narrative noting that when Israel was camped just south of Canaan and finally poised for the anticipated assault to take the "promised land" (13:1ff), a reconnaissance mission went bad, resulting in the expedition's destructive, downward spiral.

Men returning from a scouting mission reported, "The godless people who dwell in the land are strong" and "the cities are fortified and very large" (13:28). They sowed fear into the hearts of the Israelites.

Poisoned by discouragement, the Hebrews were in no condition to courageously reassert their claim in the ancestral land that had been home to them during Genesis. "We are not able to go up against the people for they are stronger than we," they lamented (13:31b). The spies "gave the children of Israel a bad report," continues Moses, noting their primary complaints: "the land devours its inhabitants… and all the people we saw in it were of great stature… and we were like grasshoppers in our own sight, and so we were in their sight" (13:32-33).

The word "confidence" comes from the Latin *con fides*, meaning "with faith." (*Con* means "with"; *fides* means "faith.") The absence of confidence dooms enterprises before they start, for *"one's attitude determines one's altitude!"* — circumstances determine nothing. Losing their confidence—their faith—the Israelites lost the battle before a single arrow was fired.

God took their lack of resolve as a religious affront: so inextricable was the good-faith relationship between God and the men of war, that the Lord construed their lack of faith in an ultimate victory as a lack of faith in Him, personally, as an omnipotent God.

Serious challenges confronted the fledgling Israelite community then—as different sorts of "giants" forever confront every generation; but problems properly met can be opportunities with work clothes. In this case the negatively predisposed cynics, who could not or would not marshal the resources necessary to overcome their naysaying inclinations, doomed themselves and their associates to an empty non-life of aimless wandering in a desolate wasteland until death claimed them. Moses tells readers that the Israelites were doomed to wander about in the wilderness until the jaded older generation dropped off and out of sight.

Moses' Authority Challenged

Though their destiny to wander resulted from their own loss of faith, some of Moses' unhappy constituents decided the fault lay with Moses' administration. It's just easier to blame someone else, is it not? In chapter 16, Moses faced a very serious insurrection. Though the rebels didn't have the courage to take on the giants, they had no problem taking on Moses.

"Korah rose up... with some of the children of Israel, two hundred and fifty leaders of the congregation, representatives of the congregation, men of renown. They gathered together against Moses and Aaron..." (16:1-3). They proceeded to tell Moses that, "he took too much upon himself," and that he was "exalt[ing] himself above" others (v. 3). Essentially, they were angry that Moses had so much authority, and they weren't happy that their lives (which they saw going the wrong way) were so heavily influenced by Moses' decisions.

Moses really had nothing to do with it. But, *Moses held social power, and thus became the lightning rod for their mounting tensions to strike.* The electrical energy, already circulating in the atmosphere, simply built up and struck against the highest, most-visible object: Moses, in this case.

In much the same way, so-called "Palestinian" people are keen on blaming Israel for their dire circumstances. This deflects their personal responsibility for building a better life and provides an outlet for the malcontents' pent-up frustrations, misplaced though they are. In this regard, I believe that the mislabeled "Palestinians" suffer their abysmal plight due to bad decisions by their leaders, and abandonment and betrayal by fellow Muslims.

It is difficult to work constructively with people who refuse to accept responsibility, but blame others for their plights. Difficult, but we must suppose nothing is impossible. That Mosaic Law requires Jews to "go the extra mile" to help the "poor" and the "alien" binds Jews to seek to do good, no matter the resistance they meet.

Readers of Numbers observe a succession of complaints directed toward Moses. The people took issue with him over a lack of food staples; his sister took issue with him over her dislike of his marriage partner; leading Israelite men contended with him when they didn't like his decisions, and just because he had authority and used it. If Moses—with his sterling character—was forever contending with disgruntled people, we can conclude that *all leaders, despite their intentions, capabilities, and decisions, will forever be the object of private scorn and public derision simply by virtue of the power they wield.* Such is modern Israel's lot, too. Police, judges, pastors, mayors, governors, presidents, generals, and the like have to absorb the angst directed at their various offices.

A person or nation in a position of leadership needn't do anything wrong to invoke the ire of others: *all the leader has to do is lead*—it's as simple as that! Conversely, the key to avoiding criticism is inaction; say nothing, be nothing, do nothing. For as soon as a leader ventures to "stand up" in any particular situation, the critics fall neatly in line behind him/her/them, ever anxious to tear apart their performance and bring the leader(s) down, personally and/or professionally. This was amply attested in Moses' experience—and many others, as well. *Might we do well to see criticism as "an occupational hazard" and not personalize it?* This biblical insight is played out from generation to generation, down to the present. Moses wasn't exempt; neither will we be—period.

Continuing in the narrative, we observe that some of Korah's angry and rebellious cohorts brazenly disrespected the lawgiver, Moses, and rhetorically exclaimed, "Is it a small thing that you have brought us up *out* of the land flowing with milk and honey, to kill us in this wilderness, that you should keep acting like a prince over us?" (v. 13). They had done this before, back in chapter 11: accusing Moses of depriving them of their good life, when just the opposite was true—he had rescued them from a life of slavery. Obviously, these people were confused in their thinking: they got it all backwards— what seems the norm for disoriented persons, then as now.

What does one do with confused individuals? Should Moses have reasoned with them? Did they need to have the facts re-presented? Should Moses have said: "Now people... *Israel* is the land of 'milk and honey,' *not* Egypt." Would having the facts re-presented to them have made a difference? I think not. The saying "Trying to reason with someone who refuses to reason is like trying to give medicine to a dead man" is appropriate here.

Because their fundamental problem was not rooted in reason, trying to reason out a solution would not be—and is not—an effective strategy. Moses was simply "acting under the color of his office," as they say in law enforcement, and because he was the one upholding the standard, he became the object of derision.

God, the "Righteous Lawgiver," was Himself the Judge who sentenced the Israelites to their abysmal fate of wandering in that inhospitable wilderness. He was the Magistrate who established the parameters within which Moses was working— and the priests by association. And He was the Mayor or City Manager who directed Moses to execute His decisions.

Aware of Moses' dilemma, God defended him: "the ground split apart under them, and the Earth opened its mouth and swallowed them up with their households and all the men with Korah, with all their goods. So they and all those with them went down alive into the pit; the Earth closed over them, and they perished from among the assembly" (vv. 31-33). Moses' supervisor—God—came to his defense and dealt with the malcontents who were unfairly and vociferously taking issue with him, inappropriately blaming him for their self-inflicted misfortunes.

Of course, being the leader, Moses even got blamed for the earthquake that swallowed Korah. He writes, "On the next day all the congregation of the children of Israel complained against Moses and Aaron saying, 'You have killed the people of the Lord'" (v. 41). To show His disfavor with the people as well as His support for Moses, God unleashed a plague in the camp, killing another 14,700 people (vv. 41-50). In sum, we observe that *leadership work is challenging work.* Fortunately, as Moses had trusted, God "had his back."

More pedestrian in nature, chapters 17 and 18 deal with matters pertaining to priests—their authorization, duties, material provisions, and the like—followed by a particular cleansing rite in chapter 19. It is to be observed that *dealing long-term with the discontented opens their caretakers to "wear and tear,"* which often affects their personal and professional performances.

Over time, this can and does lead to diminished capacity—with hazardous consequences.

Disobedience Causes Severe Repercussions
Moses, Israel's caretaker, was no different. When faced with another set of complaints, in chapter 20, *Moses himself snapped.* "The people contended with Moses, and spoke, saying: 'If only we had died when our brethren died before the Lord! Why have you brought up the assembly... that we might die

here? And why have you made us come out of Egypt, to bring us to this evil place?'" (vv. 3-5) Here again, as always, Moses absorbed misplaced discontent and personally took punishment. God told Moses to "speak to the rock" that water might spring forth from it (v. 8); but, Moses embellished the action and his doing so was charged against him.

Moses was at the "end of his rope" and nearing the end of his literal life. He was told to "speak to the rock," but frustrated with the incessant urgings of the malcontents, he gathered the people together and decided to take it out on them: "Hear now, you rebels!" he bitterly exclaimed. "Must we bring water for you out of this rock?" Moses then took his ASP baton (OK, it was his "staff"), "snapped," and twice beat the rock with it (v. 11).

His action shows that Moses went "over the edge," showing signs of his interior disintegration. Understandable as it was, this indiscretion cost him entrance into the "promised land." "Because you did not hallow Me in the eyes of the children of Israel," said the Lord, "therefore you shall not bring this assembly into the land which I have given them" (v. 12). *Unfair as it seems to be, Moses was required to function at a higher level* and his excessive display of anger and force cost him his job. Improper conduct can cost modern professional managers their careers as well, be they soldiers, politicians, police, or others.

Truth be known, *Moses was getting quite old, and a change of leadership would have been coming soon, anyway.* A new set of ears and eyes would be needed to meet the new, myriad challenges ahead.

Moses goes on to note the death of his brother, Aaron, in 20:22-29. He also pays special attention to problems and skirmishes with border countries as the new generation of Israelites approached Canaan toward the end of their tedious wilderness trek. The narrative moves readers toward the new challenges, and notes new energies among the Hebrews as the wilderness journey came to an end.

Obedience = Success

Readers note that God seemed pleased to go out with the Hebrews' fighting forces. The young Israelite army registered a variety of stellar, confidence-building successes in battle as they took on forces just east of Canaan proper. Sihon, the Amorite king mustered forces, met Israel on the field of battle, and was squarely defeated (21:21-32, esp. v. 24). Og, king of Bashan, another neighboring country, did likewise and Israel "defeated him, his sons, and all his people, till there was no survivor left; and they took possession of his land" (vv. 33-35). In the final conquests of their promised land, the Israelites skirmished with petty kingdoms to the east, bolstering Israel's confidence and reputation in the region, and prompting other regents to seek out less-conventional means of eradicating the threat the Hebrews posed.

Seeing his neighbors' armies and nations collapse in the face of the Israeli onslaught concerned Balak, King of Moab, and other local rulers—groups that resided in what is modern Jordan: "Moab was exceedingly afraid of the people [of Israel] because they were many, and Moab was sick with dread because of the children of Israel" (22:3). Believing that the Hebrews' success was attributed to "divine" favor—which it was—Balak the king opted to "think outside the box."

The king of Moab contracted with a well-known religious medium, an eastern "wise man," known to employ incantations and oracles to secure the favor of the gods on behalf of his patrons. Balak enlisted his services to be used against the Israelites. The fascinating story is told in chapters 22-24.

Balak paid a handsome price for a spiritual gunslinger named "Balaam" to come to town and curse the Israelites. The idea was to reverse Heaven's powers to work against the Hebrews. Though this might seem archaic today, it was the common understanding of ancient peoples, who saw physical contests on battlefields as religious contests to determine who had the strongest god.

Much to the surprise and vexation of King Balak, the "prophet for profit" Balaam refused to "curse" the Israelites, and opted instead to "bless" them—a posture he repeated four times. This really infuriated the king, as one might well imagine. "Balak's anger was aroused against Balaam," for he said, "I called you to curse my enemies, and look, you have bountifully blessed them" (24:10). Balaam announced that he simply could *not* bring divine aid to bear against them supernaturally, because the Israelites were protected by Jehovah God—and this was a situation that he simply could not remedy for his patron through incantations. He did prove to be worth his pay, however, for, prior to returning to his homeland, Balaam hatched a nefarious scheme to deliver Balak the desired end result—Israel's destruction. We don't learn until chapter 31 that Balaam was behind the ploy, but it almost worked.

Disobedience = Consequences
In chapter 25, Moses' narrative continues by noting that, in advance of the planned conquest of Moab, "the people began to commit harlotry with the women of Moab" who "invited the people to the sacrifices of their gods, and the people ate and bowed down to their gods. So Israel was joined to Ba'al of Peor, and the anger of the Lord was aroused against

Israel" (25:1-3). *The allure of sexual improprieties with foreign women had a more devastating effect on the Israelite army than did military contests with foreign men.* Assimilation proved to be a dread contaminate. Many fell for it. Displeased as He was by the fornication and attendant idolatry—note that in the Hebrew Scriptures, sexual impropriety and bad religion *always* go hand in hand—God raised His hand and executed judgment against the Hebrew malefactors, slaying 24,000 Israelite men as a result of their compromise (v. 9).

Balaam had concocted the scheme to employ the sexual talents of Midianite women to seduce Israelite men and then entice them toward their pagan religion, and thus away from their God who was their protector in battle. In 31:16, Moses affirms Balaam's culpability, saying, "Look, these women caused the children of Israel, *through the counsel of Balaam*, to trespass against the Lord in the incident of Peor." Balaam intuitively perceived that even if he could not get Israel's God to turn His face from His "Chosen People," the young men could be sexually enticed to abandon their God, incurring His wrath and forfeiting the benefit of His protection on the field of battle. The "prophet for profit" Balaam earned his fee with this particular strategy—but he met his end later because of it (31:8). Many men and women have injured themselves, or at least caused themselves major setbacks, in exchange for some "fast action" and an exciting "night on the town." Here now a host of Israelite men were added to the list of casualties! Tragic.

How did this happen? How could an assault of this nature successfully get past Moses' eyes and defenses?

Though known for possessing an intrepid and bold spirit, Moses proved unable to prevent the Midianite women from

Numbers

seducing his men. When the problem surfaced and the Lord directed His judgment, Moses was slow to respond. The Text specifically notes that sexual improprieties were even enacted "in the sight of Moses" (25:6). Moses did nothing, perhaps being too old or too stunned. Maybe it was something else. Phinehas, Aaron's grandson, did take action, however, and earned himself the perpetual priesthood (vv. 10-13).

Moses' sluggish response in dealing with the men's interrelating with Midianite women may be attributed to the diminished capacities that naturally come with age—for he was at the 120 marker at the time. It may, however, be more attributed to the fact that Moses himself had taken a Midianite wife many years prior. As we can recall, eighty years earlier, when Moses fled Egypt as a young man leaving the children of Israel temporarily behind, he made his way to a well in the Sinai area where he happened upon daughters of a "priest of Midian" being harassed there. Being innately noble, Moses championed their cause and wound up marrying into the Midianite family (Ex. 2:16-22). There were no Israelites around. Balaam may well have known about Moses' Midianite relationships and thought that he could exploit a possible weakness to his patron Balak's advantage. Whatever the reason for Moses' inaction, Phinehas did "take up" the matter boldly, affirming the kind of virtue necessary to put the matter to rest. Punishments were meted out and life went on for the Hebrews.

Life, of course, must go on; and, discouraging though it may be at times, *we must learn from our past mistakes, accept our losses, cultivate the urge to press on, pick ourselves up, get back in the race, and get back to work.* This being so, as the Israelites were drying their tears, a new census was ordered (26:1-65), and Israel's fighting strength was reassessed. They were, of course, 24,000 short owing to the Midianite debacle.

Before detailing the Israelites' resumed conquest of Canaan—
a battle approximately forty years in the making—the narrative
addresses some legal matters.

Inheritance laws were laid out in 27:1-11, as in chapter 36.
Joshua was singled out and ratified as the aging Moses'
replacement (vv. 12-23). Instructions for offerings and vows
follow in chapters 28-30. Chapter 31 contains a mandate to
remember how the Midianites put their women up to
seducing the Israelite men, and includes a registry of the
plunder from Israel's resulting vengeance upon them.
Chapters 32, 34, and 35 take up settlement rights in the new
land, and chapter 33 recounts the thirty-nine year wilderness
experience, followed by instructions for the conquest of
Canaan (vv. 50-56). Numbers ends with the Israelites poised
to take their God-given ancestral homeland—finally.

Summary and Lessons Learned

Numbers closes with a reminder of the deleterious consequences
of sexual indiscretion. Even considering all the Israelites had
been through, and the many ways that God had helped them,
provided for them, and saved them on the field of battle, *it is
apparent that God would not save them from themselves*—a sterling
reminder to us all that there is an ethics war we must fight.
While Israel shares the instruction to "love our neighbors," it,
apparently, is not to make love to them. Israel must remain a
distinct people, on the one hand, and respect its neighbors on
the other!

Numbers has much to commend it. Some of its best lessons,
I think, deal with Moses' frustrating professional experiences.
Holding the standard as an "enforcer" can wear on one after
a while, to be sure. Proper comportment is important. Leaders
shouldn't let the pressures associated with their vocations get

Numbers

them down. Given the position he held in the social economy, *Moses was, much to my amazement, the object of incessant criticisms and character assassinations.* That even someone like Moses would be made to endure perennial outrage and societal discontent prompts me not to personalize the angst displayed against leaders in today's economy. After studying Numbers, I am inclined to see criticism as an "occupational hazard." Forearmed with this knowledge, I am better able to deal fairly with people, and my tendency to react defensively is bridled by my realization that criticism "goes with the territory."

V

Deuteronomy

Introduction

Derived from 17:18, the oldest Hebrew name for Deuteronomy is *"Mishnah Torah,"* meaning the "repetition of the Torah." Though personally preferring the "repetition" title, I grant that the book's more common title, "Deuteronomy," which comes from the Greek words *"deutero"* meaning "second," and *"nomos"* meaning "law," has merit too. In truth, though, there really was no "Second Law"; rather, *what one finds in "Deuteronomy" is Moses reiterating the principal laws he already gave, back in Exodus 20*—thus a second telling of the first ones.

As Deuteronomy unfolds, readers find Moses formally reviewing God's principal requirements; he restates the essence and substance of the Torah and—guided by Divine inspiration—offers minor expansions for the new generation of Israelites, their being the generation about to conquer Canaan.

Deuteronomy was written after the older, original, generation had died off. Now, before he "passes on," and the new generation "passes over" the Jordan River *en route* to their conquest and destiny in Canaan, Moses must reassert for them Israel's fundamental virtues. This he does in the hope that the new generation might be inclined to grab hold of the values that would make Israel a *great* nation-state—and not just a *strong* one.

Three distinct discourses are observed in Deuteronomy. The first, in 1:6-4:40, gives a *review of Israel's wilderness journey* with an exhortation to remember the Law of Moses. The second, noted in 4:44-chapter 26, gives the better part of Moses' "recap:" *centralized worship* (12:1-16:17), principles for *proper government* (16:18-ch.18), *criminal law* (19:1-21:9), followed by assorted instructions for *domestic life* (21:10-ch. 25), and rituals for the *sanctuary* (ch. 26). The third and last discourse, found in chapters 27-30, places a premium on the needed *enforcement of law*, followed by the fresh *rededication* to Jehovah's will and ways. The last days of Moses are told in chapters 31-34, after which the book closes.

Exposition of Deuteronomy

Early in the introduction, readers learn that an 11-day overland trip had turned into a 40-year nightmare (1:1-5, esp. v. 2). That unfaithfulness has hazardous consequences—indeed, both then and now—seems the object of Moses' attention, and he sets out to make this point to the younger generation,

Deuteronomy

accordingly. The younger set had just recently survived the judgment from sexual immorality foisted upon them by Balaam. They were now poised in "the land of Moab," ready to advance and retake their promised land (v. 5).

The story of the spies is recounted in 1:6-46, during which time the young warriors were reminded that their parents opted to "turn back," fearing the intimidating size of the Canaanites, with whom they would have had to contend, one-on-one (vv. 20-46). The new crop of young Israelites, by contrast, were reminded how they were more courageous and had fared much better as a result of their faith, a faith already tested in battle on the eastern side of the Jordan. Moses writes that a loss of faith was their most formidable enemy.

To bolster faith, no doubt, Moses recounted (2:1-22) the young generation's decisive military victories over Sihon, the king at Heshbon (2:30), then Og, king of Bashan (3:1), culminating in a reminder of God's charge to their new commander-in-chief, Joshua: "Your eyes have seen all that the Lord your God has done to these two kings, so will the Lord do to all the kingdoms through which you pass. You must not fear them, for the Lord your God Himself fights for you" (vv. 21-22).

The stirring recounting of their victories, coupled with the promise to Joshua, prompted Moses to beg the Lord that he might be able to participate in the conquest. It was to no avail. The answer to every prayer request, apparently, is not "Yes." God reminded Moses that his fate was sealed and that, as a result, he needed to invest his energies in preparing the next generation—Joshua particularly (vv. 23-28).

Wanting the children to learn from the mistakes of their parents and older siblings, Moses closes with an eloquent appeal to the younger set, drawing upon their recent experiences: "Now Israel, listen to the statutes and the judgments which I teach you to observe, that you may live and go in to possess the land which the Lord God of your fathers is giving to you" (4:1).

Language such as "the Lord giving you the land" contributes toward the understanding that it is a "promised land" for the Israelites, does it not? Yet, many Bible expositors refuse to come to terms with this. Denying Jews their ancestral claim is a blatant refusal to absorb explicit biblical language, is it not? Yes, in both cases—of course; yet, Bible teachers do it with impunity. Better that a new generation of Bible scholars emerges and reclaims what so clearly is noted in the Sacred Texts. Interpreters who re-create God's story into their own anti-Jewish images can be compared to manufacturers of "idols."

Mindful of the harmful effects of idolatry and sexual impropriety, Moses goes on to note: "Your eyes have seen what the Lord did at Ba'al Peor; for the Lord your God has destroyed from among you all the men who [were sexually enticed and] followed Ba'al of Peor. But you who held fast to the Lord your God are alive today, every one of you" (vv. 3-4). Prohibitions against idols are reiterated in verses 15-16, reminding the Israelites not to allow themselves to assimilate into the ruling pagan culture—tempting though it may be.

Israel was to be a holy people—a distinct and separate people. Should they think otherwise, Moses notes, God will "scatter you among the peoples, and you will be left few in number among the nations where the Lord Himself will drive you" (v. 27). In no uncertain terms, success in the land was to be based on adhering to the religious and high moral principles spelled out in the Mosaic Constitution—*then as now.* That said, a reiteration of the essential laws follows from chapter 4:44 through chapter 12.

Deuteronomy

An exposition of the "Ten Commandments" is given in 5:1-
11:25—expanding on Exodus 20 and Leviticus 19. Over and
over in the Text, the Israelites were directed to "hear,"
"learn," and "observe" God's commandments (esp. 5:1, and
scattered throughout). Chapters 6 and 7 stress that Israel was
to "Love the Lord… with heart, soul, and mind—and
strength," a commandment so important that Israelites were
to remember it daily, even nailing reminders to the doorposts
of their houses (6:5-9). To drive the importance of not being
distracted from the Torah, they again were commanded to
destroy the enemy Canaanites in 7:17-26, after which Moses
reminded them of God's past dealings (8:1-10:11). Chapter
10:12-11:32 gives a "call to commitment," encouraging the
people to "circumcise their [own] hearts" (10:16), and
reminding them of the "blessings and curses" set before them
(11:26), and that a good heart toward God—and mankind—
brought those blessings. Chapter 12 reminds the Hebrews of
their unique religion and their need for corporate worship;
and it prescribes a house of worship, and respect for the
officiating Levites.

Much as the Israelites were to distance themselves from
pagan enticements and practices, and maintain fidelity to the
ancestral religion, they were also to guard against being
impressed by "flashy" false prophets (13:1-18). Israel must
remain distinct from other nations! The food regulations
found in 14:1-21 support the point: if they didn't eat the
foods of those around them, they would be less likely to
socialize intimately and intermarry as a result. Distance is
good! Moses reminded them of their tithing requirements
(14:22-29), followed by instructions for the "sabbatical year"
(ch. 15). Festival concerns are discussed in 16:1-17.

All through this section, and prior to his permanent absence
through death, Moses does what he can to strengthen Israel's

institutions, and buttress its determination to remain a distinct nation.

Moses discusses principles for the future governing kings of the Hebrews in 17:14-20. The king must refrain from greed and personal acquisitions, for this would be a misuse of his authority (vv. 16-17). To help curb his inclination toward self-serving, the king was to do the following—good suggestions for all who wield power: "It shall be, when he sits on the throne of his kingdom, that he shall *write for himself a copy of this law in a book*... and it shall be with him, and he shall read it all the days of his life, that he may learn to fear the Lord his God... that his heart not be lifted up above his brethren... that he may prolong his days and his kingdom" (vv. 18-20).

Need leaders handwrite a copy of the Pentateuch? It would be helpful, to be sure. But, I think a simple reading would suffice to personally acquaint, or re-acquaint, them with the Text's superior ethics. Making the effort to read Moses' Law demonstrates a characteristic desirable in any leader: an interest in getting head, heart, and arms around the biblical mandates noted in Scripture. This inclination will pay dividends in all aspects of life.

In David's Psalm 119:9, he asks, rhetorically, "How can a young man keep his way pure?" He answers the question, saying, "By guarding it according to Thy word!" Deuteronomy seems to commend the same. After accentuating the importance of being "righteous" and exercising "justice," Moses addresses a host of associated concerns, matters important in their own right.

Moses encourages generosity toward the Levites who, by virtue of their vocation, were at the mercies of the population. Tithing back then was akin to taxes today, monies paid for government

Deuteronomy

expenses, not just religious ones. *Thus, were the Israelites not to comply with the mandates* (like tithing), *the priests would suffer personally,* and also the government with its criminal justice system and army (18:1-8).

Chapter 18:9-chapter 14 exhorts the people to avoid wicked, pagan customs and priests, and to follow legitimate authority (vv. 15-22). Chapter 19:1-13 establishes cities of refuge for those who unintentionally killed someone, setting them and their circumstances apart from those who willfully and intentionally took life. Protection was afforded to the former. Property boundaries are discussed in verses 14-15.

A "Geneva Convention" appears in chapter 20, delineating the rules of warfare. This is followed by biblical particulars for unresolved murders (21:1-9). The mandate to be kindly disposed toward female captives (vv. 10-14) precedes an explication of individual inheritance rights (vv. 15-17). Verses 18-21 give drastic remedies for dealing with rebellious children, and capital punishment is the object of attention in verses 22-23. Chapter 22:1-12 discusses the proper and ethical treatment of land animals and more.

Not wanting to tax readers with excessive detail, let me just say that Moses spells out particulars for principal civil laws in chapters 16-18, principal criminal laws in 19:1-21:9, and unpacks principal social laws in chapters 21-26. Having summed it all up, Moses concludes his second discourse.

Chapter 27 prescribes public ceremonies for the Israelites to enact upon crossing the Jordan, with the "Blessings" of obedience and the "Curses" of noncompliance to be voiced and agreed to by the masses. Chapter 28 details the promises of obedience (vv. 1-14) and graphically depicts the curses of disobedience, vividly and prophetically describing the ruin that would befall Israel should the people prove recalcitrant (vv. 15-68). Moses' charge to Joshua and Israel follow, in 31:1-29, coupled with a song (31:30-32:47), and a final blessing (32:48-33:29).

Whether God dictated chapter 34 to Moses before the fact or to Joshua after, Deuteronomy closes there by telling of Moses' peaceful death, drawing attention to his memorial services.

Summary and Lessons Learned

Deuteronomy was written to recapitulate the substance and essence of the Mosaic Contract. Moses needed to tell the younger generation of Israelites the story of their ancestors, and recount the lengthy and frustrating wilderness trek. He encourages their—and our—compliance with the theocratic constitution given at Sinai, and promises that blessings will befall those who adhere, whereas curses will be visited upon those who don't. Fundamentally, this is Deuteronomy.

The attention Moses gave to leadership and justice encapsulates the message of Deuteronomy and is a fitting study for anyone who wields power.

Note the following mandate in 16:18-22:

> You shall appoint judges and officers in all your gates, which the Lord your God gives you, according to your tribes, and *they shall judge the people with just judgment. You shall not pervert justice*; you shall not show partiality, nor take a bribe, for a bribe blinds the eyes of the wise and twists the words of the righteous. *You shall follow what is altogether just,* that you may live and inherit the land which the Lord your God is giving you.

Deuteronomy

My italics above denote the premium Moses placed on "justice" for *all*—a hallmark of biblical religion and repeated by him often. The English translation of verse 20 as, "you shall follow what is altogether just," obscures the fact that in the Hebrew Text the word "justice" is actually mentioned twice—and appears superfluous at first glance.

Note the repetition when the Jewish prophet thundered, "Justice, justice shalt thou follow." The seeming redundancy draws emphasis to the importance of evenhandedness in administering civil and criminal jurisprudence—a notion that characterizes biblical religion throughout. For this reason, criminal convictions were to be secured on the basis of more than one witness: "for by the mouth of two or three witnesses shall the matter be established" (19:15-21). Judges were to "make careful inquiry" of facts and witnesses (19:18), to ascertain the truth, in order to insure balanced justice for all. Those vested with authority to manage the population are given an awesome responsibility and must be impartial in the performance of their duties—*fairness to all is the governing maxim*. How these principles feature in our culture will be considered in the conclusion that follows this chapter.

Like Moses before them, Old Testament prophets also demanded social justice in no uncertain terms. Amos, for his part, decried those who "turn[ed] justice to wormwood" (Amos 5:7), who "diverted the poor from the justice" due them (v. 12), contented simply to "tax" them (v. 11) or "tread them down" (v. 10) for their own personal gain.

"Woe to the oppressing city," said Zephaniah (Zeph. 3:1); for, it will meet an inglorious end! *God demands justice, and is not kindly disposed toward those who deny it to those in need!* Micah summed it up well: "He has shown you, O man, what is good; And what does the Lord require of you but to do justly, to love mercy, and to walk humbly with your God?" (Micah 6:8).

Man—all humankind—was created in "God's image" (Gen. 1:26) and, thus, is in possession of inalienable rights, be he Black, White, Hispanic, Asian, Jewish, Christian, Muslim, atheist, a native citizen or an alien, rich, poor, or somewhere in between. Rights due women and men include, but are not limited to, honor, personal dignity and respect, and freedom to benefit from the fruits of their labor. Injustice toward humankind—whomever and irrespective of the reason—is, by contrast, a blasphemous, disrespect toward God—and not just toward the offended person. It is a flagrant disavowal of the fundamental rights of others granted by God, and is thus emphatically eschewed outright in God's economy, a fact stressed in Deuteronomy and throughout the writings of Moses.

Conclusion

A culpable and contemptible "shoe bomber" named Richard C. Reid attempted to blow up a jetliner with a bomb in his shoe. On January 30, 2003, after being found guilty, he stood before Judge Young, of the U.S. District Court, to receive the sentence for his intended actions. In conjunction with delivering Reid's life sentences, the judge went on to upbraid the remorseless fellow.

Reid brazenly justified his actions in response, saying, "[I am in] allegiance to Osama bin Laden, to Islam, and to the religion of Allah." Emboldened as he was, he displayed no signs of contrition and refused to apologize, choosing instead to stridently offer his justification: as a soldier of Islam, "I am at war with your country."

The disgusted judge took issue with his mythic and romantic warrior image saying, to "call you a soldier gives you far too much stature. [Y]ou are not an enemy combatant; you are a terrorist!"—hardly a real soldier. "I ask you to search your heart," said the discomforted judge, "and ask yourself what sort of unfathomable hate led you to do what you admit you are guilty of doing." Then, in response to his own rhetorical

103

musings, and to Reid's obvious impenitence, Judge Young continued: You did this because "you hate the one thing that to us is most precious. You hate our freedom. Our individual freedom. Our individual freedom to live as we choose, to come and go as we choose, and to believe or not believe as we choose.... It is because we prize individual freedom so much that you are here...." Soon thereafter, the judge ordered, "Mr. Custody Officer. Stand him down." On that note, the drama ended, and Mr. Reid was taken away from the spotlight to stare at the four walls of his prison cell for the rest of his wretched life.

Judge Young gave voice to the fact that Reid's values were markedly different from our own. For us, attacking unsuspecting non-combatants is not the stuff of noble soldiering—period. By contrast, prevailing Islamic reasoning and rhetoric extols the massacres and celebrates those who initiate them. Though it is apparent that these people are not like us, it is not sufficient simply to say that they aren't like us. Rather, *it is incumbent upon us to explain how our guiding principles are distinguished from theirs*—Moses continually reminded the Hebrews of their distinctive Law—*and consider how those principles might guide us in determining how to deal with the threat imposed by such aggressors.*

Though American culture is historically rooted in Judeo-Christian values, an aggressive and emergent non-Christian secular underclass is asserting itself forcefully to push Judeo-Christian values to our culture's periphery, if not out of sight altogether. These secular humanists foist non-traditional practices (like homosexual "marriages") and disparage the "Ten Commandments" in our courts and schools; under the doctrine of religious tolerance, they uncritically accept Islamic encroachment, while stridently insisting that Christians keep

Conclusion

our religious values to ourselves and passively accept their non-religious values and immoral practices.

Should we let secular, anti-religious activists define our reality, or allow aberrant religious leaders to impress forever their anti-biblical ideas upon us? I think not, and believe we should boldly stand up, and unabashedly advocate for the Judeo-Christian values that once made our country great! This belief fueled the writing of *Guns & Moses*.

When Thomas Jefferson prepared the first draft of the "Declaration of Independence," he noted that "When in the course of human events it becomes necessary for one people to dissolve the political bands which have connected them with one another," they should articulate the reasons for that separation. He went on to note that there are separations which "*God* entitle[s] them" to forge. Foremost among the justifications for dissolving the social bonds was the belief that "all men are *created* equal and are endowed by the *Creator* with certain unalienable rights." After delineating those "rights" for all and a host of grievances, the "Declaration of Independence" closed with: "We, therefore, the representatives of the United States of America, in General Congress assembled, [are] appealing to the *Supreme Judge of the World*"... and "for the support of this declaration, with a firm reliance on the protection of *Divine Providence*, we mutually pledge to each other our lives, our fortunes, and our sacred honor."

My italics above note the civic document's appeal to a "Creator God," Himself the "Judge of the world," the One to whom subjects must ultimately reckon. It is noteworthy that *the document frames its argument in biblical verbiage*, and *appeals to God* at the source of the argument. The roots of those inclinations are discernable in Moses' writings, are they not? The modern call to marginalize Christian ethical voices in civic discourse is more the work product of revisionist atheists than it is the doctrine of the country's founders.

The Pentateuch is the spring from which our Judeo-Christian ethics emerged. It contributed greatly toward our country's social structure, our understanding of the "rules of [social] engagement" and of the "use of force" in managing civil and criminal incidents. This is evident by the mark Jewish Scripture left in our country's fathers' private memoirs and official writings. To see further proof of this, let's briefly consider our "United States Constitution" afresh, and note the biblical reflections it contains—foremost, the emphasis it places on the biblical concept of evenhanded "justice for all," stressed in Deuteronomy and throughout the Pentateuch.

The "Fourth Amendment" to the Constitution, in what is called the "Bill of Rights," guarantees *The right of* [all of] *the people to be secure in their persons, papers, and effects*," thus providing a hedge of protection against the tendency of powerful leaders to abuse those without means to hold them at bay. In like manner, the Fourth Amendment also provides guarantees *"against unreasonable searches*," noting that it "*shall not be violated, and* [then that] *no warrants shall issue, but upon probable cause, supported by Oath or affirmation*," additional guarantees against intrusive secular or religious state-sponsored powers.

The amendment finishes by noting that warrants must be specific, "*particularly describing the place to be searched, and the persons or things to be seized*." This gives more "rights" to individuals who find themselves at odds with governmental powers—for offenses real or imagined. This protection of

Conclusion

individual rights places the "Bill" squarely in the realm of biblical ethical principles, as our cursory reading of the Pentateuch showed us. Those deemed guilty of offenses cannot simply be spirited away and summarily executed under the cover of law or religion—an anarchic practice common in many countries; for cases must be built, and due diligence must be maintained to ensure that the accused are not being unfairly molested by authorities.

The "Fifth Amendment's" requirement that *"No person shall be held to answer for a capital, or otherwise infamous crime, unless on the presentment or indictment of a Grand Jury"* makes it more likely that evenhanded justice will be served, given that a group of individuals must be gathered to hear a "case," and not just a particular religious or secular magistrate, who may have a vested interest in the case's disposition. The only exception is in times of war—*"except in cases arising in the land or naval forces, or in the Militia, when in actual service in time of war or public danger"*— when it isn't possible to convene a Grand Jury.

Once tried, the person will not be placed in double jeopardy, that is, twice subjected to the ordeal: *"nor shall any person be subject for the same offense to be twice put in jeopardy of life or limb,"* much as we protect one from having to actively participate in his own defamation. The "Fifth Amendment" guarantees *"nor shall [he] be compelled in any criminal case to be a witness against himself "*—this being its most famous component. It also provides that one may not be *"be deprived of life, liberty, or property, without due process of law; nor shall private property be taken for public use, without just compensation,"* further demonstrating the high moral standard—rooted in august, biblical vision.

So as not to leave one languishing in a dungeon before trial, the "Sixth Amendment" guarantees, *"in all criminal prosecutions the accused shall enjoy the right to a speedy trial."* It then promises a *"public trial,"* to protect the accused further against malicious judges, who might be tempted to secretly remove adversaries. The requirement that the trial be heard before *"an impartial jury of the State and district wherein the crime shall have been committed, which district shall have been previously ascertained by law"* provides further protection, as does the stipulation that the accused immediately *"be informed of the nature and cause of the accusation"* so as to not leave the accused uncertain about the legal challenge(s) ahead. Requiring that he *"be* [personally] *confronted with the witnesses against him* [and] *to have compulsory process for obtaining witnesses in his favor, and to have the assistance of counsel for his defense"* are all designed to further his cause in the proceedings, not the State's.

These, and other, lofty Judeo-Christian ideals were extracted from the Jewish Scriptures; and I believe that these must remain the principles that forever guide our culture. Though they make room for others in our world, *those "others" must not be allowed to breach our hospitality and redefine our world according to their alien standards.*

For example, Muslims who live among us derive great benefit by doing so. Because our Judeo-Christian principles guarantee freedom of worship and the pursuit of life, liberty, and happiness, they have wonderful opportunities in America. Islamic nations don't reciprocate, of course, and these freedoms are not offered to non-Muslims in Islamic-controlled lands, and are not even guaranteed to all Muslims in Muslim lands. *These and other distinctly Judeo-Christian principles must be held inviolate, as they provide us with a biblically-based hedge of*

Conclusion

protection against prevailing human chaos, which comes through secularism, in some cases, and bad religion, in others.

As noted at this book's outset, Genesis begins by giving a brief telling of humanity's troubled origins, followed by an expansive telling of moral decay's entrance onto the stage of the human drama, and the tragic personal and social defilement that came as a result. Genesis, to be sure, reads like a complicated "crime scene," with a host of "offenses" noted. As a remedy for the problems, Abraham was introduced into the arena with a promise that order would, one day, be brought out of the prevailing moral chaos through his progeny. The Pentateuch shows us the work product of Abraham's faith and children.

Exodus plays out against the backdrop of a disease-infected world, hundreds of years after Judaism's founding father, Abraham. It finds the Israelites in abysmally difficult circumstances foisted upon them by a tyrannical Pharaoh. Moses, in contrast to the many wicked people around him, shows himself to have a keen sense of moral virtue and social justice, and is therefore chosen by God to lead the Israelites out of Egypt and begin reforming their deplorable social condition.

This Moses does through the revelation of God's standards for a just and orderly society, through his delivery of an extremely equitable "Law." Leviticus expands upon Exodus' legislative accounts, delineating particulars for civil, criminal, and sacerdotal regulations, and placing emphasis on ethical principles. As noted, our culture's foundation is established upon this bedrock, and must remain firmly moored there. Would that other governments were as prudent as ours in choosing this as a foundation for life!

Numbers tells of Israel's wilderness experience, and warns of "vocational hazards" associated with leadership. Moses himself was the object of derision throughout the Text, not to mention the better part of his entire career. At one point, Moses became disconcerted and "lost his cool;" his doing so reminds us of the precarious and tempestuous nature of leadership vocations—for Moses and for us all. Though Moses delivered the world's best, most equitable administrative code, he continually absorbed tension, scorn, and derision from his contemporaries. Those who wish to lead would do well to consider his life and remember the abundant difficulties. To govern prudently, leaders must resist personalizing discontent when it is expressed against them—as it often is: better to see it, instead, as an occupational hazard—something evident in Moses' writings. Lastly, the ethical mandates expanded in Deuteronomy remind us of the imperative to employ evenhanded justice (even to those who agitate us), a point that cannot be overstressed, given its centrality in Judeo-Christian ethics.

Of course, other principles can be deduced from the Torah—and perhaps will be in another book. I personally believe that simple exposure to the biblical narrative enhances ethical development. As a result, I am comfortable believing that just following along as I rehash some of the biblical principles, as you have throughout this volume, serves a good purpose.

We considered that the God who gave the people of Israel a Land also gave them instructions on how they must conduct themselves in it. Once deemed a despised, slave subclass themselves, the miraculously-freed Hebrews were required to be kind toward the unfortunate among and around them: being thus inclined was as much a religious obligation as was their keeping the Sabbath and circumcision.

Scripture says that the Jews were given title to the Land of Israel in perpetuity. Because this applies as much today as yesterday,

Conclusion

Bible readers should support modern Israel's bid for legitimacy and stability, and consider those who are bent on its annihilation as enemies of Judeo-Christian faith and literature, and not just as enemies of Jews and the modern nation-state of Israel. Just as Israel has a right to its small parcel of land, it is worth restating that Israel is also under a biblical mandate to do right by the Arabs presently under its administrative charge. Should those resident Arabs wish to be absorbed into the vast and mighty Arab cultures and nations round about, fine; but, Arabs living in an enlightened Israeli culture enjoy a finer standard of living than anywhere else in the world—the Arab world, particularly. If Arab discontents appreciate the benefits provided by Mosaic Law, and if they opt to disavow their violent ways and earnestly seek to live in genuine peace with their Jewish cousins in the Israelite nation-state, then Israel has a biblical obligation to explore ways to assist them in finding their place in an enlightened Mosaic culture...as per Moses' mandates. In any case, Israelis must continue to take pains to be just and equitable with the Muslims in their midst—or secure Divine disfavor as a result.

It is good to be strong. It is good to cultivate kind dispositions, as well. *Both* are necessary for one to be successful. For this reason, I feel that all those who wield any measure of power and influence can benefit from *Guns & Moses*. Employers, spouses, parents, teachers, school principals, shopkeepers, bankers, police, lawyers, judges, soldiers, mayors, governors, presidents, generals—and more!—can all benefit from exposure to the writings of Moses, as familiarity with His precepts helps one be firm when needed, and yet gracious all the while.

Jeffrey Seif has hit an inside-the-park homerun with his latest contribution, *The Iranian Menace in Jewish History and Prophecy.*

Iran is central in end-times prophecy. At a time when Iran has captured the world's attention with nuclear threats, Jeff harnesses both scriptural and secular evidence to support his case for the Iranian-Armageddon Connection. After a glimpse of Iran in ancient Roman and Jewish histories, you will learn the significance of prophecy in Jewish Scriptures and apocalyptic literature. Jeff's analysis is based on sound scriptural understanding as well as his conclusions from two decades of academic contemplation. This easy read will provide fodder for its advocates and critics alike.

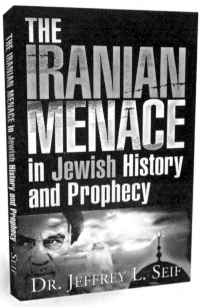

PROFESSOR ELLIOT KLAYMAN,
THE OHIO STATE UNIVERSITY

Please visit www.levitt.com to order online, or call 800-966-3377

Have Jeff speak to your church or group.

Jeff and Zola co-created our correspondence course, *The Institute of Jewish-Christian Studies.* Contact Scott in our office at (214) 696-8844 or **sphillips@levitt.com** to find out more.

*i*Network (PAX)

Does your cable company carry *iNetwork* (PAX)?

See *Zola Levitt Presents* on **Thursdays:**
9:30 am Eastern and Pacific Time
8:30 am Central and Mountain Time

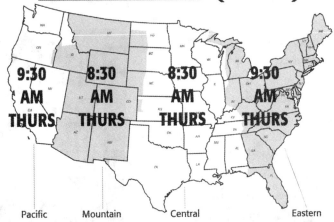

9:30 AM THURS

8:30 AM THURS

8:30 AM THURS

9:30 AM THURS

Pacific   Mountain   Central   Eastern

DirecTV–Channel 255   **Dish**–Channel 181

Check listings in your area for current airing times. Or, visit our website www.levitt.com

ABC-FAMily

Does your cable company carry ABC FAMily?

See *Zola Levitt Presents* on:
Mondays 1:00 am Eastern and Pacific Time
Sundays 11:00 pm OR **Mondays** 2:00 am Mountain Time
Mondays 12:00 am Central Time

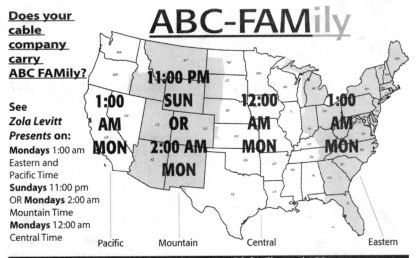

1:00 AM MON

11:00 PM SUN OR 2:00 AM MON

12:00 AM MON

1:00 AM MON

Pacific   Mountain   Central   Eastern

DirecTV–Channel 311   **Dish**–Channel 180

INSP
(the New Inspirational Network)

Does your cable company carry INSP

See Zola Levitt Presents on Wed. Morning:
6:30 am Eastern
5:30 am Central
4:30 am Mountain
3:30 am Pacific

OR

Wed. Evening:
8:30 pm Eastern
7:30 am Central
6:30 am Mountain
5:30 am Pacific

3:30 AM WED / 5:30 PM — 4:30 AM WED / 6:30 PM — 5:30 AM WED / 7:30 PM — 6:30 AM WED / 8:30 PM

Pacific   Mountain   Central   Eastern

Check listings in your area for current airing times. Or, visit our website www.levitt.com

Does your cable company carry Daystar?

Daystar

See Zola Levitt Presents on Fridays:
6:00 pm Eastern
5:00 pm Central
4:00 pm Mountain
3:00 pm Pacific

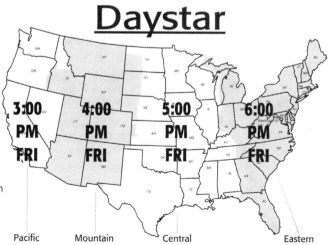

3:00 PM FRI — 4:00 PM FRI — 5:00 PM FRI — 6:00 PM FRI

Pacific   Mountain   Central   Eastern

DirecTV–Channel 369   **Dish**–Channel 263

INSTITUTE OF JEWISH-CHRISTIAN STUDIES
Dr. Jeffrey L. Seif with Dr. Zola Levitt

Complete the 12 courses below and receive a handsome diploma with your name in calligraphy! Each course comes in a 3-ring binder with an audio CD or two audiocassettes, a reading packet, and a mail-in test. We'll evaluate your tests and encourage your progress as you enrich your walk with the Lord.

A unique blend of Jewish and Christian perspectives, this self-paced program brings the seminary to you. Each course is designed to be completed in about a month.

You can order these courses through our online store at: **www.levitt.com**

Old Testament Survey — After mastering this study, you will understand the background and chronology of the entire Old Testament.

New Testament Survey — The Old Testament teaches about the garden. This course will show you the flowers!

Jewish History — Those who love history and the Jewish people will consider this one of the most fascinating courses.

History of Modern Israel — Learn how Israel became a nation in the worst of global conditions.

Comparing and Contrasting Jewish and Christian Theology — Examine key Scriptures and doctrines showing both the Jewish and Christian perspectives.

Messiah in the Law of Moses — Where and how did Moses speak concerning Jesus? This course gives the answers!

Messianic Prophecy — Fully evaluate Jesus' claim to be the Promised One of Israel.

Between the Testaments/Origins and Demise of the Pharisees — Examine what happened during the 400-year inter-Testamental period.

Judaism Today — Understand your Jewish friends, neighbors, etc.

The First-Century Church — The first Church was a Jewish one. This course examines the demise of early Hebrew Christianity.

Church History and the Jews — One of the saddest courses, yet a subject that is vital to understand.

Israel and End Time Events — Focus on the chronology of events related to the Rapture and beyond.

CD or audiocassette format:
www.levitt.com
or call 800-966-3377